CLOUD
OF DUST

A BIOSOCIAL ANALYSIS,
WHY DO THEY ACT AS THEY DO?

ANTHONY D. WALLACE I

A Cloud of Dust: Why do They Act as they do, A Biosocial Analysis. All stories are a work of non fiction from the authors and are not meant to depict, portray, or represent any particular person Names, characters, places, and incidents are either the product of the author's imagination or are used fictitiously, and any resemblances to an actual person living or dead are entirely coincidental

ISBN: 978-0692855874

Layout Design: Write On Promotions
City and State of Publication: Indianapolis, Indiana

Foreword

They Showed Up:

They showed up. This is all one would need to say when describing the Security Dads. When tragedy brought a sense of despair and hopelessness to Arlington High School, they showed up. When the number of children growing up in fatherless homes increased, they showed up.

As a former student of IPS, and now a current teacher, I have witnessed firsthand what a group of committed men are capable of doing. They are capable of demonstrating consistency and maintaining their desire to serve when others had abandoned their post. Within my life, there could have been a number of posts left unmanned. Fortunately; the Security Dads filled those voids.

Twenty four years later, I am still witnessing these men who refuse to relinquish their post. In twenty four years, they have remained loyal and confident that change is not an unobtainable goal, but a goal that is forever in view.

As I stated previously one could easily state "they Showed Up" to describe the Security Dads, however; I must add to that description. "They stayed!"

Marlon Sam: A.H.S. Class of 1995, current I.P.S. teacher.

Dedication

To my best friend & life partner Linda Ann Cheney-Wallace, our wonderful children; of course there would not have been a program without our beloved children Anthony D. Wallace II and Lena L. Wallace-Middleton.

To our beloved Wallace, Middleton & Cheney Families.

To our family and angel now in heaven George Russell.

To our family and angel on earth Dr. Jacquelyn S. Greenwood and our Arlington High School Family.

To our New Spiritual Life Christian Church Family.

To our beloved late State of Indiana Congresswoman Julia Carson who supported us from day one and worked tirelessly for our cause, which culminated with a visit to the White House as the special guest of the Vice President and the President of these United States of America.

I thank you all for your love and your support

(Epigraph)

How can we as men find peace to sleep?

How can we as down multitudes of our children creep?
How can we with good reason hold selfishness so deep?
How can we ourselves reflect and not weep?

How can we knowing God His promise keep?

How can we as men, with no remorse, sleep?

Table of Contents:

Intro for your contemplation

My mind will not allow me to recall the home going services of my father; however, I witnessed one just recently of a child who was the same age as I was when I lost my father. The child looked up at his mother and asked," Mommy is daddy sleeping?" She paused as the tears were now freely flowing down her face. "Yes baby, daddy is sleeping." The child as curious as a healthy four year old baby boy should be asked, "Why is he sleeping up there?" The mother is crying, the 10 month old baby girl on her lap is crying, the boy in all of his confusion starts to cry. The sanctuary is packed, the balcony is full, young men and women line the hallways striving for one more chance to say goodbye.

What kind of testimony is this, hundreds of young folk grieving in their own fashion? Many are high or inebriated; the smell of marijuana and alcohol filled the church. I could not help but be concerned for this child, the mother that is, and her two children. This is another episode of acquiescence; some of our people are devouring one another. Many are being systematically eliminated by spirits in the guise of law enforcement. I could not help but notice the interaction; some would say that you should celebrate the home going of your loved ones.

Many of these young people seemed to me to be seeking attention for themselves. They have this pretence of arrogance, and a total lack of respect for structure, Religion, or for God's house. For them and the law there is an eagerness to escape deep thought via anger, and to reach for their semi-automatic courage with the slightest hint of confrontation. "You don't know me, I'm crazy, and I'll go off. " The ignorance is overwhelming as I listen to this dialog, if you will, some cannot form a complete sentence. Those are the most volatile ones of the group, I think they are fully aware of their short comings; consequently they reside on a hyper level of sensitivity. These individuals are truly afraid, they are the unpredictable danger. Thus the loss of another young black man all of 25 years of age; old by the current street norm of black on black resignation.

Did this young man give any consideration to his life partner or to his fatherhood? These are questions he most certainly cannot answer now, and as always the children will pay the price. I should not judge, who am I? The eternal question is like a preponderance of base drums inside my head, "How long oh Lord, how long?" One guess is until we get it right, God helps those who help themselves, and for our men, the denial is very strong.

If men do not do what they are supposed to do the world is going to continue to change.

The human mind is not only a terrible thing to waste; it is also a tragic thing to lose. Like a drug addict and his or her addiction and an ever present craving for the fix that never seems to wane.

Like the desert dry and desolate, starving for saturation and in its' self imposed confusion tries to account for every grain of sand. The human mind is like that of a sponge, it exists to acquire knowledge. When deprived of this input there is a chemical reaction some akin to the desire of a deprived drug addict. It cries out for informational input, the ignorant in their confusion will make vain attempts to appease this wanting in all the inappropriate fashions. Their attempt to satisfy this yearning with an adrenaline rush; to inundate it with alcohol; to appease it with chemical joy, all fail in just a predictable fashion. The mind and body, working in concert, will attempt to send signals to these individuals but there is no ability to reason. Their reservoir for knowledge and wisdom was never filled and left to be dry. Just as the body will attempt to purge itself, when one has consumed an over abundance of alcohol or bad food, one will regurgitate to the point that they are drained of life necessitating moisture; referred to often as dry heaves.

The cerebrum works in like yet reverse manner, in an attempt to draw in knowledge. A condition of cerebral dry heaves if you will; the mind is trying to reach out and draw in something that is not available as the reservoir is dry. Furthermore, the ignorant ones among us, rise each day with this yearning that they cannot and do not have the understanding to satisfy. All of their attempts to inebriate or to exhilarate this crave into submission fail. They become frustrated and act upon this frustration in many individual, yet predictable ways. Some acquiesce, many become predators in their own communities, and consequently society is burdened by their plight.

As human kind we are predisposed to be inquisitive; our curiosity compels us. Should one be presented with the ultimate answer; ultimately, one would be left with a question. The answers that we seek will not be found at our conclusion; but rather, during the journey itself. I will endeavor to touch your hearts, but I shall proceed by connecting with your minds. Many of us are not thinking; consequently, our minds are like dry wells, deep, but lacking any substantial substance.

We are consumed with the thoughts of personal appeasement and selfish gain. Many of us have lost what has been our bastion throughout our history in the Americas; which has been our faith.

I was once asked a question; "Is it that life is really just too short, or is it that we simply don't take advantage of every moment we have in life?"

I was watching my favorite program, so it took me a few moments to give this some worthy contemplation. The young are oblivious to time, so they don't give moments any consideration. The teens and the immature young adults believe that all moments should be enjoyable. As maturing adults many reminisce over good moments gone by.

The middle aged have the realization of all the moments lost while procrastinating.

The advanced aged adults are simply hoping that they have a few moments left.

Now, take a few moments and consider what you just read.

Thank you in advance for your consideration.

A Cloud Of Dust

A Cloud of Dust

As a young man born into hard times
Mississippi; my family and I would have tragedy
early in our lives. The gravity of the circumstances
and those to follow; would dramatically alter the
direction of not only our lives, but all of those
around us as well.

Let me take you down home, Desoto County,
Hernando Mississippi, circa 1950; before and after
the storms; we had to go through to get out. The
truth is in these words.

Something or someone so familiar,

Chapter One:
The Legacy of George Calvin Wallace

A father to none, and an abbreviated life.

When the dust settles; it is in-discretionary in
its inundation, all surfaces are subject to its
covering. Every crack and every crevasse is
vulnerable to its penetration.   Dust in many cases
is a precursor to decomposition, or a consequence
thereof; however, in some instances dust provides

a layer of protection. Biblically; from dust we came, and unto dust we shall return. George Calvin Wallace, or that dam George as he was often referred to by family, friends, and enemies (yes, I said enemies, and George had plenty) early in his life down home in Hernando, Mississippi....Not having a whole lot of family history to go on, we don't know why George was as he was. When we would ask Granny Bernice about our grand daddy she would always respond that he wasn't worth knowing. So our family history started with George. We were blessed to be able to spend some time with momma's family yet we were still too young to get the full effect of a positive family structure. Granddad spent most of his day working the fields and Mom Mamie took care of the house and tended the garden and chores nearby. Everybody seemed to be working on something.

Uncle Alvin was young and still growing up himself, aunt Marie was momma's big sister, the enforcer, who nobody crossed. Momma, Dorothy Evelyn, worked a little bit of everywhere; even play seemed to be work down home on the farm. Now as for my daddy George, most people would have to live a life time to build up the type of reputation that George had done in just twenty five years.

There's an old cliché some men use when they're either afraid or just full of themselves, "I'm a lover, not a fighter". Well George would do both with equal enthusiasm. My uncle, Alvin Guy was the name his mother gave him. He told me a story about how he and George would hang out together before he hooked up with Dorothy Evelyn. There was a time when they visited one of the local juke joints, (local club or place to drink and dance for those of you with big city terminology.)

Uncle Alvin excused himself for personal relief, upon entering the restroom he noticed this rather large brother standing in a corner. He continued on to take care of his business. As he was about to leave this man stepped into his path and said to him," You're a pretty little fella aint cha? 'I think I'll make you mine." Uncle Alvin asked the man to move out of his way, he refused and started to undo his trousers.

At this point uncle knew he would have to fight his way out, in his words, he said, "I thought we may as well get to the truth so I cracked em wit a hard right, the big some o bitch just smiled and rushed me." We tore that small room to pieces and made enough noise 'til everyone in the juke joint was standing in and at the door, that's when George stepped up. "Bru-da" he asked, that's what we call him, "What the hell is going on?" "This big sissy is trying to make me his, that's what ain't going on." Daddy just looked at the man and shook his head; he asked my uncle if he was okay.

Cloud Of Dust

The big man replied, "He'll be fine when I'm done wit em" to which George replied "That ain't gonna happen!" The man then asked my daddy if he wanted to take his place, George told him man you already gittin ya ass whupped now why you wanna mess wit me.

Someone in the crowd yelled, "Man, That's George Wallace!" The big man paused and tried to visually measure George and said, "So, you be George Wallace? Hemmm, you not all as big as some say." Daddy stood about six foot two with weight of about two forty five. George started to walk away when the big man yelled, "Don't run away pretty boy, I can have both you bitches for myself tonight." That was a mistake. George turned around, the crowd backed off to give him room. You see this was nothing new to locals in Hernando, and the big man wasn't the first to come calling when he heard of George's Reputation. George stepped further into the room, Uncle Alvin moved back towards the crowded doorway. You see George was an artist and he needed room to perform his work, just like in the old west everybody wanted to witness the shootout but no one wanted to get hit. There were always plenty of witnesses to tell the story, but the details would vary about a country mile and the story would grow over time.

Pastor Anthony D. Wallace I

My uncle would go on to say, "There were no more words at that point, see George didn't believe in talking about it much. All I saw was ya daddy's shirt floating in the air, one punch, he hit that man so hard that when he hit the wall you could hear the wood crack."

We never saw that big man again, but there would be more. There were always more.

After that it was time to get back to one of George's other activities, on the run again. As they were leaving the juke joint that night with one of the other runners, George was doing his usual 100 mph or more when this guy started complaining.

The more he would complain the faster George would drive. Uncle said one thing he learned early on was not to get on Dad's nerves because then he would go into his stunt driving routine, hairpin curves, jumping ditches and doing 360 degree doughnuts on a two lane bridge. The more this guy would cry the lower Uncle would sink down into his seat, finally George reached down under his seat and snatched up a bottle of shine and tossed it into the air. The car was moving and spinning so fast that the bottle seemed to be suspended in the air, well that bottle got away out the window and shattered on the ground. George stopped the car immediately and put the brother out, that's where he left him, standing on the side of the road, and he said he was costing him money; "Damn George!"

Well George was quite the rolling stone. Aside from his ability as a pugilist he was quite the ladies' man, a cat dancer and he didn't discriminate. George had relations, but not relationships with his friend's girls, with his friend's wives! George even had relations with some of his cousins! I guess my daddy thought he was royalty.

That brought about the question that mothers and fathers have been asking for an eternity, "Why do good girls like bad boys?"

Momma was fourteen years old when she and George decided they wanted to marry. She insisted that they had to get permission from Granddaddy Lee Andrew. This, from what I'm told was not an easy under taking; you see George had that reputation. He was a bad boy, he was not trustworthy, and he was a philanderer. Granddad had many more adjectives to explain his distaste for my dad, but being a Christian! Well I think you will understand a father in protect mode. Granddad would call out to Mom Mamie, "Ya daughter is trying to hook up with that bad ass Wallace boy!" Mamie being hard of hearing would reply, "Who ya say?" "Wallace!" "You know the boy!" "That Damn George!"

"George ya say?" "George Wallace, hmmm,"Oh My!"

Now I'm as sure as you are that Lee Andrew and Mamie had that talk with my mother, you know the talk. Most of us at that age start to smell ourselves and just simply refuse to hear common sense.

I recall a time Momma was out working the fields and I was giving Mom Mamie a hard time. She took a swat at me and I made another big mistake. I ran out the door and down the road just far enough that she couldn't see me. I sat by the road blowing dandelions and stomping dust clouds. Dust clouds always reminded me of my daddy, even today. Oh, Brother! I remember walking down the road making dust clouds; I can recall missing George even then. I came upon this boy; I looked at him and right away did not like him. For some reason I felt that he didn't like me.

A bump became a shove and then we fought and fought, every time I thought he was getting tired he would swell up and come back at me. Now this in turn would make me even angrier and we fought on. Suddenly, I felt someone grab my arm, "Stop it right now!" It was Auntie Marie. "Ya'll gonna fight all day?"

"Boy, take your bad ass home!" "Sandy!" That's what they called me because of Papa, he could never remember my name, and the sandy one he called me. Called out by skin color, that would become a very familiar refrain also. "Get up

7

to the house before I beat the hell out of you ma self." She would say to me, "boy I guess you just met ya little mean ass match didn't you." I would find out later that the boy was my brother; damn George! Auntie Marie tells this fight story now every time I see her.

George Wallace was Hernando Mississippi's version of Casanova and thunder road, if you know the stories. One way or another; the crash was going to come, sooner or later, one way or another.

Daddy George decided somewhere in the mid 1950's that farming and running shine was not all it was cracked up to be. He decided that he would go to Indianapolis and try and find a job. Maybe the pressure from all his escapades with women and the law were weighing on his consciousness.

George left the farm for about a year, I understand that the racism in Indy was not to his comfort. You see the only time when black and white became an issue down in Hernando was at the harvest market, and at school for the few of us that went. Oh, not to forget when George was running from the law.

Daddy decided while he was away to try his luck in Chicago, Illinois and Nashville, Tennessee. George didn't have any luck finding employment; however he did manage to leave his seed in both cities.

I do believe that at about this time there was a huge exodus of black folk migrating to the north looking for fair and equal treatment, "something about Civil Rights."

After about a year or so George decided to return to Hernando, no one had to announce his arrival. There may have been some who couldn't hear him coming, but there was no doubt in anyone's mind when they saw that cloud of dust.

One day when daddy found a little time for us between runs and working in the fields he showed us how to make toys. We learned how to fashion a tractor out of a piece of wire, wheels and all. He also taught us to whittle figurines from a piece of wood.

I remember when we got our first store bought toy; it was a radio flyer wagon. It was a beautiful red with white side rails. Well, we thought it was a toy until we broke it.

Daddy beat on us pretty good, you see we were to use the wagon to fetch the water barrels from the well house up the road at Papa's.

We could play with the wagon but it was not a toy, it was a tool and not to be broken.

"You boys want to go for a ride with ya daddy?" Momma interjected, "George, No!" "These are my boys Evelyn!" Momma would say no more.

Cloud Of Dust

The one thing about riding with daddy was that you had to look fast or you would miss everything. All you could see behind you was a cloud of dust.

He would throw you all over the car, no seat belts in those days you know. Sometimes we would fly up into the back dashboard area and if we flew over the front seat he would just slam you down.

Then you would hear the siren, you could occasionally see a hint of the sheriff's red lights, but he or they in some cases were being buried in the cloud of dust. George would do a couple of steep hills and hair pin curves and then hide the car in the bushes, not that the dust wouldn't do.

There was this time we had just out ran the sheriff " again " and we were hiding in the woods, the sheriff was just a few yards away. He was very upset, he said to his deputy "That Damn George!" "We gone hav'ta do sometin 'bout tha dam Nigger."

Now Daddy George didn't appear to worry too much about the sheriff's threat, in fact he went right on making his runs. That was however the last time he would allow us to ride along. One thing our family would always do was go to church on Sunday.

I don't recall daddy ever going to church. Just above the church we could see two sheriff's cars in the ravine. We saw the sheriff and his deputy outside of the cars ranting and raving. Papa would just laugh and hum, "That dam George." Annie would ask, "What say?" Papa would answer, "God is Good Annie" to which she would reply, "All the time Papa, 'all the time."

One at a time they all started to leave Hernando, All of Georges' sisters and even Granny Bernice; they all packed up and moved away. I heard they were going to this place called Indianapolis; where was this place?

The fall of the year rolled around and momma told me that I had to go to school. "Where's that momma, 'Indianapolis?'" "No boy," she would say, the bus will pick you up on Monday, "bus?" "Yea, 'it's like a big truck with lots of seats." "Don't worry Annie will be there." Yes, my Annie was a school teacher.

When the bus arrived the first thing I noticed was the white driver, Henry, my older brother, pushed me in and we went all the way to the back. I thought that was cool. As we made our stops I felt better because all of our cousins were getting on board. The shock came swiftly as we moved further from home; the bus was suddenly filled with loud staring and swearing white children. I had never heard the word Nigger so many times in my short life, who were these people?

As we approached the school I felt much better as I could see my Annie standing out front of the building. Getting off the bus the white boys especially were on a name calling roll. Annie would say "Matthew, Isaiah, what would God say of such talk?" She knew them all by name. "You know the bees will get you for such talk." "Wow, Annie was going to whip them too!" They would reply, "Sorry, Mrs. Cathy." When I arrived at my classroom it was just like home. There were no white children in my class. I didn't like school, there were just too many people; whatever their color. In case you were wondering about the bees, Annie would pick three switches from a bush and braid them together like the girls do their hair. She would leave three spikes on the end of this weapon; she called them the bees. The first time you get hit with this thing you will know why she calls them the bees. Annie would warn you, "The bees will get you, if you don't watch out."

Change

Come Sunday the family went to church, as usual George did not go. We walked down the road to our house, we were all happy to see daddy's car out front. George opened the door, "Hey ya'll, how was church?" Momma replied, "It was a good sermon." Daddy ushered us all into the house, "How's my babies?" We all walked in and daddy closed the door behind us. Momma and daddy hugged for what we didn't know would be their last time, and walked towards their room. Momma stopped to place our baby sister Cynthia down on her bed.

That's when the moment happened that would change the direction of our family's lives forever. Daddy walked past the window, shots were fired "Boom!" and again, "Boom!" It was the loudest sound I had ever heard. At that point it was like everything was moving in slow motion, but at the same time it all happened so fast. I saw daddy falling, Momma was screaming, Glass and blood were flying all over the room. Momma was running to get to my daddy; she would fall in his blood numerous times fighting to get to him, she was screaming nearly as loud as the gunshots that had failed him; she got to him. I can remember vividly the images of my mother wrestling with my father's body. It was as if she was trying to put him back together; flailing in his blood. The gun shots had torn his shoulder off of his body; I am sure now looking back as a rational adult that George had to have died instantly.

Momma screaming for me to go and get help; and I ran moving as you would expect from this severe trauma, and being all of five years old hesitating and then realizing that I needed to move quickly ran out the door. I ran up the road to Papa's house. Papa had the only functioning telephone in our area; he called for an ambulance. Papa, Annie and I arrived back at the house. Papa had Annie to take us all out of the house; she would keep us there on the porch. We were all crying, scared and confused; all we could hear was our mother screaming. There was something that I can't explain in the sound of her wails. There are times today that I can still hear her screaming; those are the times I must stop by her house or give her a call. As we stood on that porch with Annie she prayed and cried with my sisters, through all the shock for me it was in that moment of realization that our father was gone. There you have the legacy of George Calvin Wallace; a father to none, and an abbreviated life.

About two hours later the ambulance came slowly down the road, Momma was hysterical. She jumped on the paramedics (or whatever they were called at that time) and started hitting one of them in his chest. She was screaming, "You killed him!" "You killed my husband!" The other paramedic grabbed our mother and threw her to the ground; he kicked her again and again. "Nigga don't fagit who you are!" Papa and Annie just held on to us and would not let go. I looked over on the road, I could see the sheriff's car; he never came down to the house, then he drove away. They tell me I never shed a tear.

The very next morning the sheriff came down to the house and took my father's car; we never saw him again. Momma cried all through daddy's funeral they say, I would think that was natural, but she cried for weeks after that. The whole incident seemed like one moment or flash in time, but it would not end. There was always something to remind you of the circumstance, it was like dreaming but you could not wake up. Again from this perspective I don't recall any Ministers or Deacons coming to visit our family. In modern times the churches would visit, or the community would send some kind of grief councilors to assist the family through this tragedy. The feeling was just so strange, something was not right. Granny Bernice showed up at the house one day and said to my mother, "You cannot handle all of these children by yourself." She then took Henry, just Henry, and went back to Indianapolis. We did not understand; all of the Cathy and Wallace family was angry with my mother. For some reason they were blaming my mother for George's death.

Cloud Of Dust

I don't remember dreaming much before daddy died, but since then I would dream often. Songs about missing fathers always got to me, children waiting for their fathers to return, wives and mothers burning candles in the windows. Our reality was that our father would never be coming home, never again. I think of my daddy every time I see a cloud of dust, even today.

A few months passed and Momma decided that she could no longer stand to see this house that George had built for her, or this land where he had lived and died. She decided that we were going to the city, she was going to get her son back, we were going to be a family, and we were going to make our lives work. Yes, we were moving to Indianapolis, that place we had heard so much about.

I was thinking at the time that it would have to better than Hernando. The night before we left for Indy a drunken man broke into our house. I always thought that news traveled fast in small towns but I guess this man let his booze think for him. Vulnerable woman alone in house with five small children; this would be easy picking for some quick sex. I guess he never heard of an angry woman suffering or a mother in protect mode of her children. I heard my mother scream, I stood up and she ran right over me. After a few moments I realized that it wasn't her screaming at all; it was this man. My mother had been sleeping with this cast iron skillet, she hit this fool so many times and so hard that he was running around the house and screaming like a woman during child birth. He finally managed to find the door and ran off through the field. You could still hear him crying as he faded into the darkness. She beat this brother down, turned and said "all the more dam reason to get the hell out of Hernando, shit!"

Chapter Two:
Indianapolis aka "Nap Town"

There was an Aunt in Indy, the first to offer her help; I found out later that she had an ulterior motivation. She wanted to see my Momma sleep, to see if she rested peacefully. She was of the belief that if my momma had anything to do with my daddy's death she would not be able to sleep peacefully. I thought back to the time that our father had gone to Indianapolis in search of a job. How different would things have been had he stayed in Indianapolis?

Momma put together what little she had; Granddad Lee Andrew and Mom Mamie gave what they could spare. We boarded a train and we were off to Indy. All I can remember about the trip other than it taking forever was passing over those high train trestles; we had never seen anything like this before. However I was not afraid; I used to ride with George Calvin Wallace.

When first we arrived in Indy, Once my mother was able to stand on her own, or at least away from George's family, we started a somewhat nomadic existence. Moving every year was the norm as our economic state did not allow for ownership of any kind. Unfortunately for us children and perhaps even more so for herself, Momma's strange men friends were like leaches sucking the life out of her. They not only were draining her mentally and physically, but would consume all of our resources, of which there were generally none to spare. There were many episodes of both mental and physical abuse levied upon my mother, my sisters and myself. Let me remind you that I fought with these predators on many occasion; and that Dorothy was still very young, and very immature. She had been raised to believe that a woman needed a man to care for her; consequently, she was on somewhat of a mission with the wellbeing of her children in mind.

My mother once told me that every time she had a chance for happiness that I would ruin it for all of us. I was not going to give in to these greedy pretentious Frank and Johnnies even though I knew what she was going through. This went on for a period of years before the Lord sent Herman Franklin Washington to rescue my family from this continuous tragedy. You must know by now that being a shock driven male child I fought with him too. Herman was different; no matter what I said or did he would not leave, and he didn't touch my sisters. This was a revelation for me as I would later learn to believe that he was sent by God; our lives slowly began to change, yet there was an abundance of mental trauma to overcome.

Meeting my future wife Linda was another change of life for me; although at the time I really did not have a clue. The constant moving had placed her and I on a collision course guided only by the Holy Spirit. Linda and I had attended four different elementary schools and junior high school before we eventually met and got to know each other at Arlington High School. I recall seeing her on many occasions and being infatuated yet not having the courage to speak. I know for this reason we were meant to be united as the Lord saw to it that our paths would continually cross. Getting married was particularly daunting as I was not mentally mature enough to hold up my end of the commitment. I had to mentally grow through many wayward years and come to grips with the legacy of my father, his family, and the effect that reality had on my psyche.

Unfortunately my brother Henry and my sister Janice would eventually succumb to the debilitating mental anguish that was our mental burden following the tragic death of our father. Moving forward Linda and I had two beautiful children in Anthony and Lena which would also have a role in saving my life and my soul as I would have a psychological relapse early in their teenage years. Linda and I founded the Security Dads ministry out of the realization that numerous families were suffering through the same traumatic and dysfunctional family structure that we were exposed too. Linda had gone through a childhood traumatized by divorce, separation anxiety, alcoholism, as well as physical and mental abuse for her and her siblings. Together we were armed with the understanding of all the things that should not take place within the family structure. On the fly we educated ourselves on all the antecedents and ramifications of the dysfunctional family structure and went about the business of intervention into as many lives as we and our volunteers could possibly have a positive effect upon.

This blessing provided us with the opportunity to meet an angel sent by God wearing the name of Dr. Jacquelyn S. Greenwood. This union provided the vehicle that would after 25 years of fatherhood and family advocacy, preaching, speaking, and teaching that would land the three of us in the White House in Washington D.C. having conversation in the Oval Office with then sitting President Bill Clinton. It seemed to all happen so fast, I had to remind myself on occasion that it was not all just a dream. We had affected so many lives; we had over 45,000 young and maturing adults referring to us as mom and dad. People knew of the three of us around the world; all of this brought about by tragedy, a broken family structure, and the part God appointed us to play. No brothers and sisters, this was not just a dream.

Chapter Three:
Plight Zone, State of Mind!

An image came to me in a dream, a silhouette of darkness. As the warm wind blew against this silhouette of darkness; it stood erratically still, as if to hope that no one would see. I thought of my father who I never truly knew. I asked the question, "Is that you George?" The figure replied, "I am sorry," and then vanished as if it was never there. I have already forgiven George Calvin Wallace. I have forgiven his mother. This was a woman who seemed to hate everyone; in particular Men. When queried about our grandfather she would say that he was not worth knowing. She was hurting. Grandmother had children by three different men, yet she would die with no man at her side, and she was not a widow. She had made some choices that she was not proud of early in life; consequently her burden was this hatred of her own femininity, and a hatred of men.

Cloud Of Dust

Bare with me brothers and sisters, this puzzle will come together, a jigsaw in structure; however, all of the pieces will eventually fit together.

Consider this historical piece…

It is for us the living, rather to be dedicated to the unfinished work of those who fought here, and so nobly advanced (Lincoln). History will tell that President Lincoln's motivation wasn't necessarily based on what he thought was in the best interest of the slaves; but rather what he considered to be in the best interest of the Union. Over 650,000 Americans gave their lives during the Civil War, and many more during the Civil Rights Movement to assure everyone would have an equal opportunity. Thomas Jefferson once said, "To expect a people to be both ignorant and free is to expect something that never has and never will be." Education, our new Gettysburg, begins in the home, is nurtured in the classroom, and is manifested throughout life. We are all aware of the toll that fathering deprivation has taken on our family structure; and consequently our communities.

The Security Dads program was organized to tackle the problem head-on. The purpose of the organization is to end this trend of Father Absence; 'the greatest scourge on society in our time, as it contributes to every form of latent and dysfunctional tendency known to mankind." By providing this; "The calming educational and directional intangible a father or positive male role model provides for a child's psyche that cannot be duplicated." The focus of the organization is to help implement fatherhood and mentoring programs. Security Dads Inc. helps develop and maintain educational training opportunities for parents, guardians, concerned community members, corporations, churches and schools. Emphasis is placed on the fatherhood initiative to not only influence the child but to motivate other mothers, fathers, young, and older adults in need of proper life models. We are promoting positive fatherhood and overall family values. There is a direct correlation between father absence, academic and social failure. The main goal of the organization is to connect children and young adults to positive adult male influences, in order to increase their opportunities in the areas of educational and social achievement.

"We must reduce the inequities in the most needed and neglected areas."

How can we as men find peace to sleep?

I am left with this query concerning certain people of both majority and minority status who have found themselves in leadership positions. What is the source of their motivations? Does one become an advocate for the oppressed and the underprivileged; or does one believe he or she has finally arrived and seek to live the good life and maintain status quo. Over the past four decades here in the state of Indiana and in the city of Indianapolis in particular; we have noticed an unfortunate trend.

There has been a continuous downward spiral of spiritual, moral, and ethical values on the part of many children, young and older adults. These individuals have no loyalties to anyone and are only inspired by their most primal instincts; greed, hatred, and lust. The idea of an education has been reduced to an intrusion or the last bastion of slavery being forced upon them. All while we have witnessed a historic number of people of color in leadership positions. To mention a few offices held; State House of Representatives, City County Council, and the Presidents and Directors of the major philanthropic or endowment organizations, all held by people of color. During their watch they have funded numerous so called help organizations, many of which have made significant contributions to society; many have not. Now after decades of moral decline and break down of the family structure and ever increasing racism, homicide, rape or child molestation, robbery, burglary, substance abuse, incarceration, and the utter refusal to except an education, this is where we stand.

The federal government has provided states with what they have titled a "Criminal Justice Grant." The effort pushed forward by the Indiana State senator who happens to be a Caucasian male. His ethnicity aside, this needed to be done; but don't lose site of the original query. The money from this grant was distributed to all the same groups or individuals who were on watch during this three or four plus decade freefall. The question is; can we realistically expect to see a difference in attitude or action from these sedentary groups or individuals than we have seen in the past. So in pondering the query brothers and sisters of color and your Caucasian counter parts that happen to be in leadership positions; I ask, "Exactly, what is your motivation?"

As the men, black, white and other continue in their bazaar pattern of denial, and the children who are left to their own devices spiral downward, I offer you this consideration. Devoid of the wisdom that comes from the instruction of the fathers, how will they learn to reason, rationalize, and deduce in a cerebrally demanding twenty first century? Who will teach their children and the children thereafter?

Think about this…

The curtain rises, enter the clowns, the puppets are all in place.

The crowd does not fear the clowns they are laughing at them, only in desperation do they receive any consideration. A danger to themselves' mainly, and others should they find themselves caught in the crossfire. Their lives are the residuals of continual oppression; and the break-down of family. We must also consider the effects of Father Absence, the apparent government abandonment, and of the idea of a formal education. Another contributing factor is the fact that our faith foundation has deteriorated. They have no true belief, nothing to hold them morally or ethically bound. There is no fear of consequence as many have made incarceration a rite of passage. Consequently, multitudes of them have cowardly, and some unknowingly acquiesced. You can't oppress an entire people for hundreds of years and not expect it to have an adverse mental and societal effect. Considering the current state of our youth; and the contributing variables, is this just a slight variation from where the expectations were to begin with.

Collateral damage: this plaque has crossed all ethnic and socio-economic lines. Malcolm X once stated, "It was just a matter of time before the poor and the children of the oppressors become subject to the same injustices as those who are being oppressed." William Jenkins once stated that, "Of those who would run from the plaque, many carry with them the same contagions from which they flee; consequently they spread this debilitating mind-set everywhere they land."

"There is a need and a spirit and a man at the beginning of every great human advance. Each of these must be right for the particular moment of history, or nothing happens" (Coretta Scott King).

I believe sister King was trying to say that we need Jesus, we must return to our religious heritage and move forward on faith; but as biblically stated we must put some works with that faith.

That thought brought to mind the following experience.

The high was incredible; it was as if my feet were not touching the floor, I was levitating. I just let myself go and let the spirit move me; it was such an overwhelming feeling. All that I noticed before, both individually and collectively started to blend. There was a smell of lavender as I walked into the room, ever so subtle, almost undetectable. There just enough fragrance to affect my senses; I could almost feel myself walking in a garden. The flowers and the foliage all take shape as they were carefully and skillfully set to accent the room. The colors of the tapestry, royal purple trimmed in gold. The colors in the choir members' robes match the colors in the sanctuary with five golden stars all coordinated to maintain a balance across the pulpit. Suddenly I was all alone. I knew why I was there, but something else was happening. My heart started to race, the emotion just took over, and I started to cry.

I do not see them, but I can feel the congregation moving in all around me. The choir starts to sing, "Jesus," "Oh Jesus," 'whenever I call you, your name is the same." That was the song they sang at both my sister's and my brother's home going. My church family knew what my reaction would be. They were all there to support me, just as they had been at the funeral service itself, my blessings are in abundance. The monitors are all glowing as the message of the day scrolls by, you hear the deacons start to pray as devotions open. They pray for the church, for the community, and they pray for our Pastor.

The Pastor enters the sanctuary; he kneels in prayer as the choir concludes the devotion services. He approaches the pulpit, turns and calls my name. "Reverend Wallace and I have had some in-depth conversation." 'My sermon this evening will be about family, and the calling that the Lord places upon you when he blesses you with a child."

"There is a sacrifice that has to be made by you," 'both of you," "Both parents." The ultimate sacrifice was made by parents, think about it." "The first trinity is of the Father, the Son, and the Holy Spirit." "The second trinity is of father, mother, and child." "As you read your Bible and you reflect about that moment upon Calvary, remember that Jesus was not the only one who suffered." "As his parents looked upon those proceedings they too would suffer." "You have a responsibility as a parent to sacrifice some of your earthly desires to ensure that your child has what he or she needs." "As the scripture reads, 'Raise up a child in the way he is to go, and when he is old he will not depart from it." "Yes it is not only a blessing to be a parent, it is also a calling." "So in your selfish confusion think back to the ultimate sacrifice." "Our father so loved the world that he gave his only begotten son." "Do you believe?" And the Pastor goes on to conclude his sermon. "And whosoever believeth in him shall not perish, but have everlasting life." Our father did all of this for you, "for you!" with the hope that you too, would believe.

The Pastor begins the great invitation, I must compose myself. As a minister it is my responsibility to welcome new members and pray for those who want prayer. I can feel the floor beneath my feet now; I join my fellow ministers of mercy below the pulpit. Tonight the entire congregation comes forward and we all pray together. Thinking back on the night, I believe that one of the true test of faith is in watching your loved ones home going ceremony. That is also the price of longevity, if you are blessed with long life you pass this way numerous times, and it is only by faith that you pass this test. I thank God every day for my wonderful family, and I am willing each and every day to make any sacrifice for them. By faith I know I will be blessed for having been a blessing. My eyes are wide open as we all go our separate ways. All I can think about was the feeling of freedom, having truly let go. I walked in the garden of my mind and I could smell the flowers, ever so subtle, almost undetectable. "Man, what a rush!"

Chapter Four:
A Matter of Consciousness

As we have witnessed the scourge of father absence and the devastating after effects; we have surmised that this is one of the greatest scourges on our society in our time. This condition leads to a plethora of latent and dysfunctional tendencies which are having a negative global impact on mankind. There is a mental stability that a father brings to a family the average mother alone cannot establish. Research has shown that there is a direct correlation between father absence, social dysfunction, and relationship failure. These boys and girls in search of that intangible find themselves mired in a state of chaos. The Columbine, Virginia Tech shootings, the Ferguson Missouri, and New York tragedies, and other such tragedies were not the beginning, and they most certainly will not be the end. This tragedy doesn't end with our children. An unhappy child grows up to become a bitter adult; there will be a reckoning for us all.

Cloud Of Dust

The greatest contribution that the average citizen can make, not only to these United States but to mankind, is to become the best parent he or she can possibly be. When one studies the fatherless rates, the education, and crime rates the correlation should be obvious. A wise old philosopher once said, "A society that leaves the responsibility of raising a child; particularly the male child, to the mother is a society on a road to destruction." This concern needs to be addressed and given a very high priority level. As we are already behind in the cause and affect that it is having on our communities. While we were watching our young men, we failed to notice that our young ladies were fast going down that same disastrous road. According to the (National Fatherhood Institute) there are over 75 million children under the age of 18 in these United States. Over 48 million, roughly two thirds do not receive proper attention from their mother or their father.

Approximately 26 million children, about one third of the youth in this country, do not know or have never met their biological father. Over 80 percent of men and women who are incarcerated in America today come from fatherless families. Children, who live absent their biological fathers, on average, are more likely to be poor, experience educational, health, emotional and psychological problems. They are more likely to be victims' of child abuse, and engage in criminal behavior than their peers who live with their married biological mother and father (National Fathering Institute).

Early intervention into the lives of both dysfunctional children and parents is needed to stop this downward spiral. "For a child, failing academically as early as the third grade should be a warning to both parents and educators that more attention is needed" (Abigail Thernstrom). As for parents who are young or ignorant as to what their responsibilities require of them, then we must make them aware of the resources available to them.

For example there is MiddWall Consulting Services; a Christian Family owned business that emphasizes parental participation at all levels of child rearing. MiddWall services are proponents of positive fatherhood and over all family values. Their consultants are willing to train families and organizations to establish and maintain advocacy groups. The federal Government over the last 15 years has established and subsequently defunded P.I.R.C.'s, (Parent Information & Resource Center) in every state in the union. They had programs such as the "Indiana Academy of Parent Leadership." This was a vehicle that was teaching parents to become the best educational advocate, not only for their children, but for all of those in their school, community, or social group. The

National and Indiana state "Parents and Teachers Association," (PTA.Org), is another resource that will open doors to many other like opportunities for parent and child. Through collaboration, the federal government and corporate America have established "School to Work," programs. The companies' partner with community schools in what is called "Adopt a School," whereby the employees are assigned a student to mentor. This is a kind of internship or job shadowing program. The youth are introduced to a variety of positive life experiences while they learn the responsibilities and expectations that come with the daily adult work routine.

Fathers programs such as "Security Dads," have been established and set up in schools, churches and community centers to provide mentors to, "not only the youth," but to other mothers and fathers and individuals in need of proper life models. Organizations that understand the need to intervene early also understand the necessity of having the parent, guardian, or mentor involved in this proactive effort to salvage the state of our youth.

While doing research on this or any subject, I find that you most continue to focus on the topic. Whether your search is on the internet or at the library, explore key words, remain patient and rational. You may try using a dictionary to define the wording you are using for your query. It may be necessary to make phone calls to some public services and ask clarifying questions. I would not deny any method of inquiry; the results are the only verification you need. Working as a team, during brain storming sessions, I find the dialog to be very stimulating. I am a firm believer that conversation enhances ones' thoughts. Reading and keeping ones' self up to date on current events can be a bonus when you need to do research on any given subject. "Being a committed parent may be your most important social, physical and spiritual contribution to the future leaders of America. Be wise about it. Invest yourself and your time in children and you won't be disappointed" (Dr. Ken Canfield of the National Center for Fathering).

Dr. Canfield believes these trends and facts most lead us to a new resolution, "There is a great cause in which all of us – women and men, young and old – need to be engaged: encouraging men to be effective fathers, and connecting all fathers with their children. It is a quiet struggle against an invisible foe – Fathering deprivation, but it is every bit as crucial and intense as any war our nation has ever known. It's no exaggeration to say that every future generation depends upon how we respond to this Opportunity."

Dr. Eugene White, Blueberries, No Rejects. Where it concerns Education in these United States of American the tendency is to withdraw funding from the public educational coffers, however the expectation for achievement is not only unchanged, it is heightened. In the words of Dr. Eugene White, former Superintendent of the Indianapolis Public School system, "we continually expect to get more with less, and then wonder why we are falling behind."

Recently I was requested to attend the annual Indianapolis Economic Club luncheon. I was not told why my presence was requested, however the invitation came from Dr. Eugene White. Since I know the good doctor well enough I decided to walk out on faith knowing that any and all expectations for me would be revealed in good time. I arrived at the Indianapolis Convention Center Sagamore Ball Room a good 45 minutes prior to my appointed time, immediately I was greeted by Mr. John Doe of the Indy Economic Club. Mr. Doe explained that the purpose of the gathering was an annual function of the club highlighting a current need within our community. I was invited because of my work with children within the Indianapolis Public School system, and consequently my connection to the key note speaker, Dr. White. I was privileged to be seated at the head table along with Dr. White and other dignitaries; it was a wonderful networking opportunity for me. The lunch was delicious; however I savored the conversation more so than the roast beef. Dr. White was introduced. He stepped to the podium, he paused as he peered over the top of his eye glasses, and with his deep raspy voice he greeted his audience.

Dr. White started his address with an analogy. He made reference to a gentleman who had made his multimillion dollar fortune through his sales of blueberry ice cream. This gentleman was addressing an audience of admirers when the question of ingredients was raised. The question was asked by a little elderly woman who introduced herself as a retired public school educator. Sir, "how do you go about selecting your berries, what if they are not ripe enough, over ripe or just plain rotten?"

The gentleman responded with a smile and with all the confidence that his successes have afforded him stated, "If they are not ripe enough we send them back, if they are over ripe or rotten we throw them out, we only accept the best blueberries as ingredients for our ice cream, that's why we're the best in the business." He smiled and waited for a response that I am sure he never saw coming. The elderly educator comparing blueberries to children then replied that through all her decades of teaching she had to except them all as they were. If they were not ready, if they were too advanced or if they were just plain bad, every one of them were to receive an equal opportunity at education, and I prayed every day that the ends justified the means.

My point is sir that even I could claim to produce the very best were all of my ingredients also the very best, half of your work was done before you started. Dr. White peered over the top of his glasses once again and paused for effect. He went on to compare American educational priorities with those of China and India. Did you know that in China they have more children in their accelerated classes than America has in their entire school population? Did you know that in India if you are in school you were in college prep? The expectations are that high! Did you also know that in each of these countries there are no special needs children enrolled in mainstream education? You will not find any children mentally or physically limited enrolled in these schools. Did you know that in these countries if a child should become a behavior problem that they were immediately removed? Dr. White went on to stress that our graduation and dropout rates are not that far off from what they have been historically. In our past young people would drop out and go on to factory or farm work, unfortunately those opportunities are no longer available. More people are being affected by this fallout and we are scrutinized by the media more than we were just a few decades ago.

Dr. White elaborated on the breakdown of the family unit and the fact that more families placed a very high priority on a formal education in years past as compared to many parents today. He would go on to stress the discontent of many about taxes being a burden and the fact that cutbacks in educational spending is always at the top of the list. He stated briefly that it makes more sense to pay for education than it does to pay for incarceration. Good, bad or indifferent we have to accept and deal with all of our blueberries, life affords us no other option…

The doctor made his point; I found the purpose of the speech to speak to a very worthy cause. The blueberry analogy was well used for we don't have the option to leave any child behind. Dr White was very strong not only in presence but very strong in his oration. I didn't notice any obvious weakness with the exception of the large note paper that he carried. His dress was impeccable and his presentation style managed to keep the audience's attention. His movement was subtle with limited gestures and his pauses were timely, when he looks over the top of his glasses everyone freezes in anticipation. Dr. White's vocal tones were very good and he always managed to inject just enough humor. He then questioned the audience in the rhetorical sense which makes them feel interactive.

"We continually expect to get more with less."

The history of American school reform (Tyack and Cuban, 1997) shows an unfortunate tendency to adopt fashionable programmatic "solutions" to deep educational problems. One viable and well supported alternative to Payne's framework is the "funds of knowledge" idea of (Luis C. Moll, Norma Gonzalez, and Cathy Amanti) that developed and put into practice theories based on the premise that all people are indeed knowledgeably competent, and their life experiences had given them that knowledge.

They purpose that the educational process can be enhanced when the teachers actively learn about the life experiences that their students have had. We should consider this "funds of knowledge" approach, creating connections between home, school and community. Building a partnership of mutual trust and collaboration between teachers and families will benefit all children, and consequently society. In order to find a solution to America's achievement gap we all must do some self examination. It is unrealistic to expect our educational institutions to educate our children on their own. The parents must prepare them properly or far too many will unfortunately be left behind. We must also be honest and work on our many manifest and latent dysfunctional societal tendencies. The actions of our children Black, White, and other, are all conditioned responses to a stimulus beyond their control.

The response to this sometimes overwhelming stimulation varies, for some it is acquiescence. They have resigned themselves to this impoverished mindset and feel that they can no longer compete with the larger society. Others feel that they have been mistreated and become angry, however their anger has no direction and they tend to lash out at those closest to them. The children are affected by these differing reactions, combined with societal influences that have resulted in broken homes, and the fact that many of the parents place no value on education takes us to new levels of desperation. There have been countless lives loss and dollars spent on the latest fads or miracle cures in education. Let us not be influenced by this notion of a culture of poverty, our denial has become institutionalized. We need to work towards collaborations with parents, church, community organizations, and political movements to ensure all peoples basic human rights. We, as adults, must think outside of that proverbial box. Every future generation will be affected by our response, or lack there of to this opportunity.

We should be intelligent enough in this 21st century to understand that there is no Medicine Man.

Chapter Five:
M.L.K. Acquiescence

Not all, but far too many, have resigned themselves to their doom. My heart burns as I witness the signs of total resignation. There are different signs as some surrender in their own fashion, or should I say in comfortable fashion. They have become very adept at following; however, they will vehemently deny this assertion. There are white flags flying all over this land, and some will object to this notion as well. One example is the young and older adults and misguided youth with their sagging pants. I am sure that many of them see this as some statement of rebellion. I ask you, is it so much your intent when sending a message, or is it more in the way or mindset in which the message is received? Some perpetrators refer to this as more of a fashion statement.

The at large community, from my understanding, views it as a statement of surrender. They have resigned themselves to the fate or mindset that they can no longer compete with those in the larger society. Allow yourself to ponder this for a moment; in the minds of many who matter they see signs of a great movement or mindset coming to an end. Lowering their trousers below their buttocks is a sure sign of resignation, representing the surrender of a historic mental and physical crusade for total equality and freedom. Consequently no one feels the need or obligation to give them any consideration let alone any respect. As I was reading of W.E.B. Dubois, "The Souls of Black Folk" I came upon many thoughts and few conclusions. One is that we as black folk should know our tails very well; fact is we have been chasing them for hundreds of years. We speak not nearly as often as we should of the widening achievement gap or educational under achievement. Our concern should be that we have allowed our children to suffer through unneeded hardship by essentially giving up on ourselves.

One question I am left with is this, "Is there so much of an achievement gap, or is there more of a wisdom gap?" We are guilty of not educating our children on their African or American heritage. These children in turn have grown up to be parents who have perpetuated this lack of interest in a formal education into a mindset that fosters failure. This is a state of mind that insures dependency upon a government that is all to willing to allow for such failure. They continue to try and remove anyone with a progressive mindset from their newly defined superficial black culture. Living out stereotypes assigned to them by predators, opportunist, and racist both black and white.

One prime example is the entertainment industry; some have apparently sold their souls, while the confused ones of us defend them. They in turn go about their business poisoning the minds of America's weak adults and children. They are the Racist few and the Criminal crew; their programming is not complete; as designed it will lead them to defeat.

The Last: Grand Jury verdicts; essentially the process of hypnosis which precedes a desired diagnosis.

The Journey: African Americans should be the most educated of all ethnicities yet many rebel, particularly men, against the structure of faith. We rebel against the structure of education. We rebel against the structure of governance; consequently we become subject to the very structures we rebel against, no hope, no wisdom, and no peace.

The First: In the frame of political correctness society wishes to dismiss the consideration of slavery, when slavery is the root cause of all inferior and superior ideologies.

Close and lock the cage door before you leave, but by all means whatever you do, don't turn off the lights. Insecurity raises rebellious rages, broke back institutions and procrastinating solutions, their consciousness is clouded because our apathy allowed it.

I was informed by a confused young brother that I was no longer of the culture; ergo, my lack of understanding his refusal to except an education.

In regard to ones cultural background one must first understand the definition of culture. As defined in "The American Heritage dictionary, Second College Edition" (Houghton Mifflin). Culture is defined as; The totality of socially transmitted behavior patterns, arts, beliefs, institutions, and all other products of human work and thought characteristic of a community or population. To put it plainly, its enculturation, or acculturation, most of us learn from our life experiences and influences. Our cultural background has affected us in so many ways both directly and indirectly, not only in the way that our people responded to it but also in the ways that others have responded to us as well. History tells us that most people base their opinions on what they have learned from family or those in their immediate environment.

African American; this was the label that was placed upon us.

We will have to improvise on some readings and words from our past. Although we have considered tracing our roots, we have to date not put forward the effort. From a geographical and historical standpoint one would conclude that they are the descendants of the first constructive versions of man in recorded history. Mother Africa as some refer to their ancestral home land was home to the first builders this earth has known. Architects and mathematicians, some structures still stand today. Our ancestors tell us we were born of Kings, Queens and Mighty Warriors. Unfortunately, our history would also lead us to believe that slavery was very prevalent in ancient times. Many of us were sold into slavery by our own relatives, but there were just as many of us who were shanghaied or kidnapped as the slave traders made their way or pursuit through Africa.

Because some Americans assumed superiority and privilege, our people were condemned to a life of forced servitude, lying, lynching, rapes, beatings, and murders which continue in the twenty first century. Now all this at one time was written into law, that our people were less than human (3/5 rule). Therefore, they or we were not privy to any consideration that would be considered inhumane treatment for any other race. To avoid conflict during the Civil Rights era, Rev. Dr. Martin Luther King decided that a peaceful proactive approach rather than reactive was the only way to survive this endeavor. Even then we witnessed the devastation of an evil, hate filled, and ignorant mindset. Many Americans of all ethnic groups gave up the ghost at the hands of a very oppressive and single minded white America. The individual opinion was very important. Their desire was to build a united mindset with as diverse of a makeup as possible. In order to remonstrate and survive Dr. King understood it would take individuals with a much disciplined will. They wanted the wisdom of experience as well as the innovation and freshness of youth. As with any group of people looking to work together some concerns will arise that could hinder our progress.

Differences in personality, education, work ethic and personal beliefs were

just a few examples. One obstacle that proved very difficult to eliminate was a clear definition of freedom. Some of us would accept anything with just a promise that they would be left alone. Yes equality would have its price; earlier in history Booker T. Washington had a plan, according to W.E.B Dubois that had too many concessions. Freedom at any price is not freedom. Now has this affected us? Yes! It has affected us in a very profound way.

This influence has led me to make statements such as this, "You cannot oppress an entire people for hundreds of years and not expect it to have an adverse mental effect." Hence the answer to a question that is frequently asked in today's culture, "Why do they act as they do?" Which brings to mind this quote, "Don't criticize them; they are just what we would be under similar circumstances." Abraham Lincoln, (Carnegie).

Our father was murdered before our very eyes as we arrived home from church one Sunday. A case in the opinion of some that did not deserve an official investigation. Although the sheriff did show up and take our fathers car. Our mother was just 14 years old when she was married and had her first child. After the death of our father, mother decided to relocate to Indianapolis Indiana. This began a life of poverty, discrimination and dysfunction that cost us the lives of our Sister and our Brother. There were no grief councilors or ministers called in to console my siblings and me. This was emotional turmoil that we had to find our own way to overcome.

As I stated earlier our brother and sister could not handle the reality of our situation and they succumbed to it. As we moved on through life I do believe that God intervened, or perhaps he was schooling us for our ministry. I met my wife at the very young age of 15. Of course, at the time we had no clue of the magnitude of change we would experience. The change at first was subliminal, and we resisted the change out of fear and ignorance. There were times when the boy in me would out pace the man I was destine to become. Again I would falter. Through these experiences there were always two constants, "God and my wife." My wife and I began to discuss the differences of ethnic groups, religions, politics, and other influences both positive and negative on the motivation of men, women, and children. We watched and listened to all the visual and verbal influences that were prevalent in our society. As we continued to read and educate ourselves we eventually started a family of our own. We were always watching them I must confess, our contribution to this world God bless. Our hope is that they are content, into this earthly hell that they've been sent. While parenting our own children, we couldn't help but notice that there were always other children present. Asking questions as children do, they reminded me of something that I had read.

"The most primary and essential way that knowledge is exchanged is through human contact, that's contact between those who know and those who are to learn" (W.E.B. Dubois). What we noticed was the prevalence of father absence, and the hunger that our children had for that stabilizing blessing that a father brings. Through this revelation we found our mission, which is kingdom building one child at a time. For all of those who would be Kings and Queens, and then some. We have become warriors for their cause.

Through our conversations we were trying to understand and explain how the similarities and differences of our cultural background have contributed to the currently dominating American culture. From a personal stand point I see our current society as one that is very resistant or reluctant to accept differences in any form. The three prevailing motivators are the same for those who have, and those who do not, greed, hatred and lust. Some have a tendency to rebel against anything that represents structure and equity. The questions of civil rights are continually reduced to an individual appeasement. Those who have been blessed to taste the fruit have continually sought to distance themselves from the misery of their roots. This new status changed their priority to a mindset bent on assimilation into the prevailing majority. History has shown us that these mindsets are not fostering overall societal good and that these selfish attitudes are affecting those who are governing our country. One of the main reasons why we are suffering the way we are today is because of our failure to learn from lessons of the past. One can explore a world of wisdom in black and white, "read!"

"I will not speak ill of any man," and I will speak all the good I know of every man." "Any fool can complain, criticize and condemn, and most fools usually do." "One needs character and self discipline to be compassionate and forgiving" Benjamin Franklin, (Carnegie). While pondering compassion and understanding; I gave consideration to the few differences and the many commonalities we share as fellow human kind. Are there enough resources for all of mankind to live comfortably?

This is reminiscent of the old Star Trek television alien nemesis referred to as the Borg. "We are not one you, we will make you, one of us, resistance is futile, you will be assimilated." Their mission was to assimilate everyone into their likeness and way of reasoning. In this new globalized economy; if the corporate complexion does not mirror a diverse workforce, the survival of this business may be in jeopardy. This is how things have changed; this new multicultural environment has eclipsed the corporate world and opened up a dialog that America has been avoiding far too long. One can hope that the words of the dreamer [Rev. Dr. Martin Luther King] may finally be realized; "That a man will no longer be judged by the color of his skin, but by the content of his character."

Chapter Six:
Tyranny of Self

"Through all of my struggles I have found the beauty of me, God is watching and the devil has finally let me be" (Macy Gray).

America, America, how proudly we fail. How would you define the gang mentality of this day? I am sure that at different times throughout our history there were any numbers of groups formed for many reasons. They were formed out of desperation, rebellion of some sort, or for any number of positive and negative motivations. So what is the motivation of some of our modern day gangs? They go about terrorizing their own neighborhoods, predators of old women, men and children. They are slowly killing their own families by pushing the oldest and latest versions of chemical joy, marijuana, crack cocaine, heroin, and methamphetamine to name a few. They are robbers, rapists, and murderers, who by their own actions have labeled themselves as cowards whether they are sagging or wearing a badge. Coward by any other name; however, in local communities they prefer the label of gang.

Cloud Of Dust

My acronym for a gang is a Generic Anomaly of a Narcotic Generation. Let us start by definition: Generic; relating to, or descriptive of an entire group or class, not having a trademark or a trade name. Anomaly: deviation or departure from the normal or common order, form, or rule, abnormality, irregular. Narcotic: A philosophy likened to a drug that dulls the senses, and becomes addictive with long term use, of or pertaining to narcotics and the effect of their use. Generation: A group of individuals regarded as having a common, more or less contemporaneous cultural or social attribute. Many are addicted to this American materialism with greed, hatred, and lust as their primary source of motivation. These young and older men and women are self appeasing, highly temperamental, and the men have very strong feminine tendencies. They are encouraged when in the presence of like thinkers, however with the slightest pressure they respond with unreasonable passion and many by proclamation and others with their semi-automatic courage; by any other name.

They are devoid of structure, refuse to attempt to acquire a reasonable level of education, and have no true understanding of the concept of brotherhood. Poverty and shame shall be to him that refuses instruction. They are angry for many reasons; one of which is their own ignorance. They lash out at anyone or anything that reminds them of their own frailties. The wisdom of the prudent is to understand his way, but the folly of fools is deceit. Many of them have become scourges on our society wrought by the combinations of oppression, privilege, ignorance, and the flight of the father figure. Consequently they have a strong dislike for older men, particularly black men. This in itself is a true irony for young African American males; you hate what you will become, deal with that. Promiscuous men; not all black men, on the other hand are in total denial, many of whom lived their lives out in total irresponsibility. Boosting of their many conquests of our women and using this as a statement of their manhood.

They are guilty of spreading their fatherly seed to the wind, and then denying the child, declaring that the mother was no good because she was too regular with other men. So with no emotional connection to the mothers they refused to accept their many children. Many men become better fathers to their second families than to their first off spring leaving in the wake an abundance of scornful mothers and confused youth. These men who walked away; fathers who are not fathers, are just as guilty as any perpetrator of oppression or injustice. They are as guilty as any corrupted politician, police officer, thug or gangster, who very well could be their sons. Many men today are still excusing themselves, refusing to accept their fatherly responsibility. They claim that there is nothing wrong with these children; "we did crazy things when we were young and we turned out fine." This from a gentleman; (loosely termed) who has 6 children that he knows of, but has not been a father to any of them. While he works a modest job and is living pay check to pay check, he refuses to watch or read the news.   I must elaborate on the fact that many women have played a role in this downward spiral as well.

They have used their femininity as a tool, a weapon, and a reward for so long that they have been bitten by their own tails. I heard an ignorant statement recently, a woman when asked about men marrying women with children, "shoot lets be real, everybody has at least one child,' 'there ain't no such thing as a virgin no more, this is 2015, duh."   When an ostrich buries its' head in the sand the dirtiest aspect of it is still exposed.   As with the simplicity of a beast of burden; an ass cannot bear any significant cerebral weight.   Let me change direction as I am sure in this new politically correct frame of mind we would prefer not to speak of anything controversial; perhaps is it too late?   For years the mothers held the families together; unfortunately, the men remained promiscuous for so long that many women started emulating the men.   Man sharing, neither he nor she wants to be reminded of the fatherlessness and poverty rate, or the rate of incarceration, or the A.I.D.S. pandemic.

They definitely do not want to accept any responsibility for the yearly homicide or murder rate. This is societal sin, black on black sin, by any other name, sin. There is a saying by Martin Luther King concerning men and women of any particular race or group who expect to be given respect when they have placed themselves and their personal and financial gain before the welfare of their decent men, women, and children. He probably referred to them as Americans.

I am compelled to share with you the continuing saga of racism, and gang mentality within the minds of the political leadership of this country. The leadership of this country failed to hear the cry of the people of color. They maintained their prejudice until their own children and grandchildren began to recognize their treachery. The leaders of this country then refused to hear the cry of their own children; consequently, we now have a President who is a man of color. The main goal of many politicians now is to discredit the ethnicity and the man the people elected to serve into the highest office.

The leaders of our country fail to accept just who it was that elected President Obama into office, their own children. African Americans comprise 12% of the population, Hispanic Americans make up 13% of the total population. That's a total of 25%, now consider all of the individuals within both groups who could not vote, and those eligible who did not vote, the percentage is then greatly reduced. Still they continue to maintain their prejudice; their own children and grandchildren are tired of their elders treacherous and hate filled mindsets. I pray for all the children of this racist few and those associated with criminality; that the sins of their fathers will not be visited upon them.

Cloud Of Dust

We need to work together so let's try this…

I have belonged to several social groups or organizations that have had profound effects on my life to this point. I do consider them special interest groups as they are all in the public service category. My wife Linda and I founded the organization of Security Dads Inc. in 1989. Our motivation was the devastating effect that absent fathers were having on the lives of our children, and consequently on our society. Our mission is to replace this missing link and restore at least some resemblance of what I refer to as the second trinity of "Father, Mother, and Child."

The Indiana Center for Family, Schools and Community Partnerships was a natural progression for us. The F.S.C.P. is the State and Federal arm of assistance to educate parents to become better advocates for their children. My wife Linda was at one time the Associate Director and I was the Fatherhood Consultant for the partnership center. The center on a federal and state level is referred to as a Parent Information and Resource Center. As the leadership of this organization slowly disintegrated from ministry to mockery and into a more self-appeasing mind set we decided it was our time to move on and reestablish our ministry as fatherhood and family advocates.

As pastor of the New Spiritual Life Christian Church along with my pastor and Daughter Lena L.

Wallace-Middleton, my wife, fellow Ministers, Elders, Deacons, and Deaconess, we strive to live up to the biblical reference of our responsibilities as Ministers of Mercy. There is an educational aspect to this calling as churches and schools are at the core of our communities. This is an opportunity for each of us to serve and lead by example and deed. In the establishment of a community the first building blocks put into place by the families are the church and the school house. By the same token the first signs of a community on the verge of collapse are the removal of the school house, the church, and the structured family.

The breakdown of the family, which is the anchor that represents a productive community, has hastened the failure and thereby doomed many a community currently teetering on the brink of collapse.

The historic consequence of such a collapse is the flight of the more structured citizenry leaving behind a remnant of a socially ill and lethargic minority to usher a once thriving community into a corridor of blight.

Community is not the inevitable result when people live in close proximity to one another. The associations that form a community resemble that of an ecosystem where the complex interactions depend on a few sources for sustenance as vital as air, water, and sunlight. Degrade just one of these resources and the ecosystem is vulnerable to systemic breakdown, so too are communities.

The integral parts of, and active participants in a community, like sunlight upon an ecosystem, is the family, the church, and the school house. These are basically deprivations of a child's rights which carry with them long term consequences that effect a child's potential for full and harmonious development of his or her personality. Not to mention their rights to social development, education, and an adequate standard of living. Neither the community nor our children need a Jack Kevorkian assist.

As I reflect on the similarities and differences between my family and myself I am pleased at the thought of the upward mobility that we have achieved. My family has evolved from a time when education was not a consideration, to a place where education is the expectation. Religion was the lone escape from the daily work routine down on the farm in Hernando, Mississippi. My family's income was generated from farming produce, cotton mainly, and vegetables. My grandparents were strictly farmers, but my father ran moonshine and any other advantage he could take by hook or crook. Our area of residence was actually in Desoto County, Mississippi. Hernando is a suburb of Desoto County. These were simple times, "circa (1950)," if one had a plot of land, a tractor, a truck or a few cows and pigs you were living large. Our main source of sustenance was what we generated on the farm; we also raised horses and chickens.

There was no true political participation by our family at that time; I believe we were content to survive the numerous Klan functions. One would like to believe that there is a world of difference between those days in Hernando and our lives today and that mankind has evolved. The more some things change the more they remain the same. Racism has become institutionalized over the years following the civil rights era, but the desperation continues as we have separated ourselves into differing social classes. This stimulation and the death of my father affected my attitude and my behavior as a child, yet has had a very different affect on me as an adult. I have gone from being a very angry and radical young man, to a person who believes in the goodness of his fellow man.

Hernando Mississippi (1958), I was 4 years old, my memories of these times are vague. I understand that my parents would attend school occasionally between planting and harvesting seasons. They both went through the sixth grade, which is where they met. There were no similarities from then to now as far as education goes; it was not a priority at that time. The crops were the beginning and ending, as the winters were long and desperate if you had a bad harvest. George would use that as his reasoning for running moonshine, although he would make runs whether the harvest was good or bad. This is where he ran afoul of the other runners the Klan, and the Law, which in some cases was one and the same. He had other bad habits that angered a lot of husbands and boyfriends, not to mention some young women that wanted more of his time. When my mother Dorothy Evelyn, met George Calvin Wallace there should have been a sonic boom. My mother from what I was told was a quiet child of fourteen years of age, and my father a rowdy young adventurer. There wasn't a rule made or a law written that George didn't break. George would go on to alienate most of his family and friends. If this wasn't bad enough he would also anger the Klan and the Law. When the family arrived home from church one Sunday afternoon in 1959, as we entered our house George was gunned down right before our eyes. The shots came in through the window, George died instantly. We don't know for sure even to this day who murdered our father, and there was no investigation. Just another dead black man, it changed our family forever, and Mother never attended church again.

In 1960, mother decided she couldn't take Hernando any more; she packed us up and moved to Indianapolis, Indiana. We weren't ready; our minds were still filled with the image of our father's mangled body. We were Southern Baptist I am told, however I don't recall any grief counseling or ministers praying for our mental health. We were desperate and poor;

we were so poor we (Prayed Often for Other Resources). Living on welfare and assisted living my siblings and I were forced into school unprepared, which put a very bad image of education in our minds. The racism in school was overwhelming; made worse by the fact that the black children were as prejudiced as the whites because of our light complexion and where we came from. My Mother is a very attractive woman, the men in Indianapolis were lining up at the door. I took it upon myself to save my mother from these bums, but that angered her. My older brother and sister under me were becoming criminals and my mother seemed oblivious.

My attitude was very bad; I fought every day and with any body that crossed my path. I was stronger than most because of my anger, young men would always challenge me as we moved from one neighborhood to another. Gangs were not a problem until about 1968, when I first noticed young men carrying guns. In 1971 I transferred from one high school to another and things started to change, there were a few young ladies in my life. There were some that would leave me because of my temper, I never physically harmed any of them, but I scared them into believing that I would. I met a young lady ironically about the same time my mother met this particular guy. She let me know in no uncertain terms that if I wanted to be with her things were going to have to change. I wasn't a bad student at the time, but I was just getting by. I improved my grades over the next two years and managed to graduate on time.

I married this young lady in 1974, my mother married in 1977. We lost my sister and my brother to the streets, they both died bitter and unhappy. My step father Herman, adopted my younger sisters and sent all three to college. My Mother, Herman (we call him pops), my sisters, little brother, and I talk often about the desperate life that we led. Each of us now have children of our own who have college degrees and are encouraging their children to be the best they can be.

We believe that the differences in our lives today are the circumstances that shaped and molded us into child and family advocates. We have witnessed the scourge of fathering deprivation and the devastating affects it has on the family structure. A bitter child will grow up to become a very angry adult. We can give testimony to the traumatic and debilitating mental affect of witnessing a murder of someone close to you. There are children going through this shock treatment routinely, as they grow up to repeat these ungodly acts against the greater society. We have learned first hand of the power of faith, will, and strength of the human mind. I would encourage every individual to pursue faith and education to the highest level possible for them. I listen as people down play religion and wonder if I could have made it this far without a belief that there is a better place and we will see a better time. No one at any time or place should have to live in poverty; this world is fruitful and we can over come our greed for the sake of our fellow man.

The heads of state need to practice politics on a different level and live up to the true definition of their offices as public servants. I am a different person today because of my experiences and the fact that I would not give up on my family. The greatest contribution that my wife and I have made to this world is the fact that we were the best parents that we could be. My children, who have their degrees, are proud of their mother and father as they pursued their degrees. To that end we feel that we are, and will strive to remain, upwardly mobile.

Chapter Seven:
Psychologically Responsive....
Inez Beverly Prosser

As I was pursuing my degree I found that the more I read in Psychology the more I believe this teaching should be mandatory for all people. Inez Beverly Prosser informed us that the effort to become the man or woman one wants to be; one has to bear in mind that enculturation plays a significant role. I believe the more aware one is of this influence, the more likely it is that one will not succumb to this socialization. Sexism as with any other form of bias are mental hang-ups an intelligent people should be able to overcome. As for male roles we have evolved, the bear is no longer in the yard. The role of provider and protector in many cases applies to the female head of house hold. If a man believes that showing compassion and nurturing his loved one's is a sign of weakness; he would learn through these teachings this mindset is a truer sign of his insecurity.

The African American masculinity issue is no different than any other ethnic group reaction would be under similar stimuli. I believe that the more demonstrative a man is in regard to his masculinity, the more fragile is the masculinity in regard to the man. The issue is not defined by the fact that slavery happened; but rather by the fact that oppression continued. Black men talk of this often because it is true. They also speak of it as if the black woman did not have similar experiences. There is a need for understanding from many throughout our society. We need transcendence, which is to move beyond the traditional roles or limitations we have placed upon ourselves. Should there be any judgment made; let it be defined by the content of one's character, and not by gender, hue, or preference.

In ministerial discussions we focused on sexuality; as tender a subject as race, in which we all could benefit from some open dialog. We would gain from setting our own set of sexual values; however this would entail some serious consideration. One should consider morals, ethics, pregnancy, STD's rather than quenching one's sexual thirst. Responding to the pressure from one's peer group and the overwhelming influence from the media can lead to a life of confusion and misery. One needs to learn to enjoy his or her own sensuality and sexuality and the difference between intercourse and intimacy. We have a contemporary crisis on our hands with the AIDS virus; which unlike people does not discriminate. This virus and all forms of STD's should give us particular concern for the youth as sex has become another rite of passage for them. Our children are experimenting with all aspects of sexuality and respond to every query with;

"I don't understand the problem, it's just sex." Ignorance or selfishness has led to a preponderance of sexual decadence such as incest, date, or acquaintance rape. These acts are reprehensible as you take away one's freedom of choice and betray their trust. I would compare them to a mental slavery in the effect that you undermine or destroy their will.

Sexual harassment is another form of disrespect and abuse of power or influence in many situations. It diminishes the choice of the individual and makes for a hostile working, school, or other environment where the attention is unwanted. An individual either male or female has the right to not be assaulted by continuous unwanted sexual oriented behavior. Let there be no misunderstanding, unless the individual verbally states differently, "No means No!"

Our conversations continued on to focusing on choosing an occupation or a career. This is a dream of childhood as one is regularly asked, "What do you want to be when you grow up?" Unfortunately for many it is just a dream; as necessity leads many to except any job they can find to make ends meet at the time of their need. For the more fortunate ones who are able to afford, earn, or gain in some way higher education, then career choices can be explored. Taking into consideration an individual's abilities, interests, values, and self concept; thereby charting a career, occupation, job, or work path. I found the personality types to be a very interesting tool in the process of deciding on a career. The desire is to find a career or job that is meaningful; as this early opportunity will shape one's attitude about work in general. As for my job; I believe I have a personal responsibility to the citizens of Indianapolis. This civic responsibility not only gives meaning to my efforts but pride in doing the best that I can. Each time my company receives recognition for outstanding service I take it personal. Some of my fellow employees seem to have a problem with the company not sharing more of the glory. I suggest to them that they reach and grab it for themselves. The testimony is that through all the economic turmoil being experienced by our nation and the world, our employment has been consistent.

I will take that as a pat on the back and share my opinion with anyone I feel is in need of mental pick me up. Another reality today is the average career will last roughly 6 to 8 years, so changing careers in early and midlife is something one has to plan for. At the same time one has to plan through these changes in setting up resources for his or her retirement. Finally in considering a well balanced life one needs to create a plan for work and recreation.

We need recreation for peace of mind. We read in earlier writings of the effects or results of a sedentary life style. We need diversion from the daily grind of our occupation in order to replenish our bodies and our minds. Just as exercise for the body and stimulation for the mind is a building process; so too is recreation and relaxation. We as individuals are mainly responsible for making our lives and our work meaningful.

Peace of mind; wellness in my opinion, is a quintessential statement or testimony of one's mental and physical equilibrium. Is it possible to achieve a totality in physical and mental balance, and have the mindset to maintain this harmony? If one is a perfectionist and views any slippage as a sign of failure; what would be his or her reaction? Personally I would set a high goal, shoot for the moon, and not settle, but be willing to accept an orbit around my goal. In other words there is no perfect state of wellness, as we will visit many stages of what we consider mental and physical wellness as we age. I imagine that life itself could be a major distraction to the individual seeking that perfect harmony.

I am a believer in traditional health and the medical advancements we have made over the years. However the holistic health attitude of mind and body has its' merits as for the connectedness, you surely cannot separate one from the other. One should make the conscious choice to do all one can to maintain a healthy mind and body. That includes going to the doctor (come on Obama) and taking advantage of all the miracles of modern medicine.

Under the consideration of taking responsibility for your body; I felt a real connection. As I was approaching middle age a few years ago my older brother died of a massive heart attack. Our father was murdered as a young man and we had no family health history to draw from; so this became my history. I have always been physically active; however I was diagnosed with an abnormal heart rhythm as a young man. Needless to say being a little older and wiser, along with the death of my brother, gave me a new perspective on my physical well being. I am blessed to have been married to a registered nurse for 43 years as of January 17th, 2016; who also has a very good relationship with our primary care physician. The two of them have prepared me very well for this middle stage of my life.

Spirituality for me has been a key ingredient to my mental stability. I have witnessed many tragedies in what seems to me a very short season of existence. I was born in Hernando, Mississippi during a very racial period in American history. Not only did my family and I witness and survive the murder of my father; but my sister was murdered after we moved to Indianapolis. This reality I am sure has had a direct effect on my direction in life today. Years of dysfunction, misdirection, and unfocused anger on my part would follow. The stress of these considerations; some self imposed, some external led to years of sleep deprivation. I found the reading on emotional upset and susceptibility to negative consequences to be true. The environmental sources of stress weighed heavily on my psyche. Before I slipped into a psychosomatic phase of emotional illness, I was reminded of the reality of our Lord and savior Jesus the Christ; I had a spiritual awaking.

Cloud Of Dust

When I met my wife in 1971; this was the beginning of a transformation I believe the Lord had planned for me. I did not elaborate fully on my life story; however I feel he had to drain me to get me where he wanted me mentally. Love was an integral part of this preparation. I had to learn to let my guard down and love myself in order to not only receive; but to give love. This would take quite a few years I am not proud to say, but I am a much better human being because of the trials I survived. My spirituality and my wife are the reasons I have survived what could have been a train wreck of bad decisions, and a dysfunctional life style. As for the authenticity of love and all of the myths, barriers, and misconceptions; there is a process that has to develop over time. What is the basis of this love; is it just a physical attraction? There are so many intangibles the average couple does not consider; consequently many relationships are doomed from the start.

The challenge of forming an intimate and meaningful relationship can be a daunting endeavor. The key word being relationship; which requires differing levels of commitment and communication. First giving consideration to both individuals who agree on what it is that they want and need. From experience I find that these considerations are not discussed until they present themselves. The seriousness or maturity of both parties is revealed at this point which raises the question of self awareness. Do you know yourself well enough to know what it is that you want, what you need, and the difference in the two considerations?

I believe most relationships hinge on compatibility. There is an old saying that one should not attach themselves to someone above or beneath them. Now I am not totally in favor of all myths and tales, however I try and consider each one and judge it on its own merit. Many are based on experience and sound knowledge and as many on biases or prejudice; weigh the knowledge and use the wisdom. As with any cognitive and emotional concern one's enculturation will weigh heavily on ones decision making. Ultimately how couples address anger, conflict, and confrontation, will determine the durability of their relationship. With that statement I am reminded of the importance of communication in all circumstances of human condition.

I have had many opportunities to mentor to both gay and lesbian individuals, being a Christian Minister and true believer I cannot agree with their relationships. What we can agree on is mutual respect and civil courtesies that should be exchanged between all humankind. Any faithful and religious person who thinks differently should continue to study his or her faith as it teaches us that it is not for us to judge. When counseling I grasp their hands and let them know that I respect and care about them up front, and that should be a mutual bond of understanding. After that I treat them as I treat all of my children and associates who happen to be gay or lesbian. Evidence of their understanding is the interaction between them and myself thereafter, I have thousands of young men and women who all refer to me as Dad Wallace.

Chapter Eight:
Wisdom of the Prudent

God's children who are afraid of being different from the world around them lose the power of their testimony to God. The wisdom of the prudent is to understand their way; but the folly of fools is deceit. Poverty and shame will be to them that refuse instruction. There are numerous aspects of human development, including physical, cognitive, social, moral, and personality development.

Throughout a life time an individual will develop many different skill sets, beliefs, habits, and witness numerous physical changes. Plato and Aristotle had differing opinions on learning. Are humans born with certain innate knowledge and abilities, are they more influenced by the learning that occurs through the five senses (Carpenter and Huffman 2008)?

There are varying opinions on developmental psychology, nature versus nurture, continuity versus stages, and stability versus change. There are some very critical periods in one's lifetime; sensitivity to certain stimulus will shape an individual's future development. This influence will come from personal experience and from observation of others. I agree with the paradoxical theory of change; self awareness and assertion, as opposed to conformity just to fit into a common fad or popular mind set. I really believe that my studies in psychology, sociology, and theology have been enlightening experiences; and I look forward to more research and the dialog that comes from it.

As I read more personal stories; and we all have a story. I could not help but reflect on influences in my life that have shaped my direction. I have read of the integrationist perspective that develops from an individual's personal predisposition and from experiences within the environment. When it comes to personality development Erik Erikson (1950) was one of many who developed a theory of psychosocial stages. I won't list them all here, however a few of them seem quite obvious to the thinking mind. Sex, gender, and culture come to mind, also greed, hatred, and love. Genders; aside from the obvious physical differences have a myriad of cognitive and biological changes during early stages of life. At an early age level enculturation weights heavily on an individual's future point of view. There are five basic personality traits; openness, conscientiousness, extroversion, agreeableness, and neuroticism. Dubbed the big five, also referred to by the acronym O.C.E.A.N., these five traits come up repeatedly during personality testing. Testing leads to such theories as the psychoanalytic, psychodynamic, and the Freudian slip, referred to as the powers of the unconscious (Carpenter and Huffman 2008). Many human beings are oblivious to the subliminal influences, or programming, on their mental point of view.

Where am I now? I would like to believe that at the age of 61 I have attained a certain level of, not just knowledge, but wisdom. As summarized earlier; paradoxically, we find ourselves when we are secure enough to go beyond a preoccupation with our self-interest and become involved in the world with selected people. I focused on the statement that crisis encompasses both danger and opportunity. In normal development critical experiences influence the choices we make in later stages of development.

As I read of autonomy and psychological emancipation; I had to ask myself if I was in harmony with both my inner and outer worlds. I believe that I am, however I do look forward to further research. That consideration left me with this thought; I must learn to challenge my inner parent and my inner critic and shape my own destiny (Corey and Corey 2006).

Consider this: Three of the major contributors to personality are the brain, neuro-chemistry, and genetics. As one ages through many stages of growth from childhood, puberty, adolescence, to adulthood, the ages of 3 to12 are the more formative years. Will the child or the adult be more motivated by the pleasure principle; immature, impulsive, and irrational; when primitive drives build up the id seeks immediate gratification to relieve tension? Will he or she be more influenced by the reality principle; super-ego, morality issues, defensive mechanisms, rationalization, or repression?

When the attempts are made to intellectualize in its search for self-actualization, will it truly understand the importance of the self concept? For example; a child raised by an individual who is a child themselves, are they destined to be a mental cripple? In most cases if there is not some timely intervention from a reasonable, rational, and responsible source I would say the answer to the latter question is yes. That is just my humble opinion based on life experience; however I believe there is ample evidence to support my thinking. I also believe that a child's parent's level of educational achievement, moral standing, and the environment they provide will determine the child's level of motivation, determination, and ultimately his or her destination.

Let me remind you again; Security Dads Incorporated was conceptualized initially as a safety piece and deterrent to inappropriate behavior at Arlington High School functions. During this time, and from prior experiences as we interacted with our youth, we noticed a profound lack of structure and basic upbringing. My wife and I decided at that point that positive male role modeling and proper mentoring were missing ingredients for a great number of our youth. The affect of "Fathering Deprivation" was and continues to take a gigantic toll on the mental state of our young, and our society as a whole. The Mission of the Security Dads program is to provide a positive adult male influence into the lives of not only the children, but other adults in need of a proper example to emulate. There is a small nucleus of fathers, 7 to 10, who were present at Arlington High School during the day. This portion of the group would be categorized as "Primary," because of the closeness and passion for our mission that has developed over a period of years. The entire Group at one time numbered up to 155, many who couldn't attend during the curricular day was present for most after school and special activities.

There was however a total understanding of our ministry. This has resulted in a change in life style for many of the men involved, so in that respect we can also be defined as a "Reference Group." The world that I have experienced as a result of this program has helped me grow both personally and professionally. I have become a motivational speaker and a trainer of trainers. I have advanced in ways that I could not define until I was introduced to the study of social psychological sciences.

The Indiana Center for Family School and Community Partnerships was another step in my maturation process. The purpose of the F.S.C.P. is to provide leadership and resources for the parents of the state of Indiana. A spin off from the Security Dads referred to as the "Fathers Too" initiative. The center's staff and I have traveled state and country wide with what we call the Indiana Academy of

Parent Leadership. A branch of the centers many workshops designed to train parents to partner with the community, school staff, and administrators for a better educational experience for all children. The center's staff consisted of 10 young ladies including my wife and daughter, who have made this a heartfelt ministry. Three of the ladies gave up better paying jobs in order to be more productive at the center. We are touching and changing lives, especially our own, from both a personal and professional standpoint. This organization would fall into both the "Primary and Reference" group category.

As a "Minister," at Greater St. Mark Missionary Baptist Church, I was truly proud to serve in that capacity. My previous pastor asked me to consider my calling a number of years ago. I decided against it. My reasoning was that I would be cheating the congregation because of my work schedule and time spent on my ministries with the fatherhood initiatives. He would except that reasoning for about a year, when he called me into his office and stated that I had much to offer in the way of leadership. He referred to me as an evangelist and stated that he expected me to answer this calling. I admitted to him that I did indeed feel the calling; he stopped me there and said your training begins now. After prayer and discussions with my wife and my children I went to the pastor and asked what it was that I needed to do. He said study the Bible and you will make yourself approved. Before I exited his office, he said classes will start on Wednesday. I am sure it is needless to say that this has had an enlightening affect on my personal life.

Professionally, I do believe I have been in training in one way or another for most of my later childhood and adult years. My responsibility as a Minister is to serve God by being of service to my family, my pastor, my church family, and to my fellow man. This organization I would also categorize as a "Primary," and as a "Reference" group.

In summary we found that the groups that we have associated ourselves with have much in common. Charles Horton Cooley, (1902) coined the term "Primary Group" to refer to a small group characterized by intimate face to face association. These "Primary" groups are all small in number as the definition goes, but all very large in affect on our social makeup. The closeness of these groups, in the source of their motivation and the strength of their dedication, gives me energy. Cooley defined a "Reference Group" as 'any group that an individual uses as a standard for evaluating themselves and their own behavior." There have been numerous inquiries from local, state, federal government, and institutions around the country and abroad about the Security Dads and F.S.C.P. programs. Fathers are disproportionately the non-custodial parent; with no commitment to the mother it affects the relationship with the child. The fatherhood programs are there to help build up the family and community through education. For all such programs there are interested people and organizations searching for solutions to the crumbling moral fabric that seems to be reaching pandemic proportions on a global scale. Biblical history tells the story of the church and "Deacon Ministry" from the first seven to the modern day servants. Another opportunity for those concerned with our humanity to lead by example. With that in mind men we have a responsibility!

Chapter Nine:
Parents Left Behind

Throughout the history of man, the mantra has always been the same. There were times when mankind found them-selves in a situation of disease of epidemic or pandemic proportions. Mother Nature at times has created catastrophic conditions that would cost the lives of thousands, and the mantra remained the same. Unfortunately there were also the times when man, through his own ignorance, pitted man against man in situations of war. When the fever was at its peak, the fort was about to be over-ran, or just before the ship would sink; the captain would declare this mantra, "save the women and children first!" Here we stand in the 21st century at a time when ignorance reigns.

After the demise of millions of families and the flight of just as many fathers we find ourselves mired in the midst of three generations of latent and dysfunctional tendencies. Three generations of children who were raised by children who value education even less than life, consequently many have displayed a genocidal mentality. The current generations of problem children and young adults are the products of those parents who were left behind.

In 2001 our President introduced legislation entitled "No Child Left Behind." The intention was to create a national environment in which all children would have an equal educational opportunity. The fallacy in this case was and is that for all children to have an equal educational opportunity, all of their parents would have to be privy to the same blessing. N.C.L.B. is merely the latest version of federal legislation enacted to hold educational institutions accountable on education reform. The state of Indiana, as do most states, has its own version of education reform legislation entitled Public Law 221. Both N.C.L.B. and P.L. 221 have parental components written in; however there are no provisions or guidelines written on how to gain and maintain parental participation.

W.E.B Dubois stated over a century ago that, "The most primary and essential way that knowledge is exchanged is through human contact, a contact between those who know and those who are to learn" (Jenkins, p17). I feel it safe to assume that this contact and exchange of basic knowledge should come from the child's first and most influential teacher: the parent. Without this basic structure or foundation as a child approaches his or her formal educational opportunity, he or she, is and sometimes irreversibly: left behind. The parent or parents in these situations are at times equally immature and apathetic, fighting demons of society, or of their own making.

Speaking of these parents; I am compelled to share with you the opinion of Mrs. Ruby Payne (2003). Mrs. Payne has a very condescending take on our impoverished and uneducated mothers and fathers, black, white, and other. The reason we are all inclusive is because we have never known poverty to discriminate. Our mission is to show them that they too have what it takes to not only move beyond their current situation, but to reach back and help those coming up behind them. However, according to Mrs. Payne, this is a colossal waste of time, "They are where they are by choice." Ignoring influences like being born to a teen mother, death or absence of a father figure, single parenting, bad politics and business practices. Other influences on the American psyche include our constant battle with ignorance, apathy, racism, and oppression. Mrs. Payne would give credit to none of these as having any variance on ones impoverished state of being, but attributes it all to what she refers to as a culture of poverty.

As these children flounder the school systems are busy treading state and federal governmental waters. They continue to search for new ways to transform education with new or renewed initiatives to improve the academic achievement of struggling and uninterested students. The latest catch phrases are

"Rising to the Challenge," and "Community Schooling." They are touching three bases with initiatives in literacy, numeracy and science, as well as instituting small schools to reduce class sizes. According to school officials "the purpose of small schools is to improve students' academic, social and behavioral performance, to reduce the dropout rate, and to connect students in a more personal way with school" (IPS). They also speak of curriculum enhancement, student support, and continued professional development for all staff. I support and applaud them in their efforts.

We must keep in mind the toll that family break down has taken on the collective psyche of our society. We should also be aware of the role that fathering deprivation has played in this destruction of our communities. "Fathering deprivation is the greatest scourge on society in our time, as it contributes to every form of latent and dysfunctional tendency known to mankind. The calming educational and directional intangible that a father or positive male role model provides for a child's psyche cannot be duplicated. A priority should be placed on the administration and parent organization to help implement fatherhood and mentoring programs. Emphasis should be placed on the fatherhood initiative to not only influence the child but to motivate other mothers, fathers, young and older adults in need of proper life models. There is a direct correlation between father absence, academic, and social failure. School systems must make every effort to promote and nurture parental involvement in order to connect children and young adults to positive adult influences. Society must help supply the recourses needed to maximize every child's opportunities in the areas of educational and social achievement.

There is a recipe for a world class school system; it comes in the form of the second trinity, mother, father and child. It is unrealistic and unfair to think that any school system can raise and teach any child after not being properly prepared by the parents. Children who have not been taught to read and count prior to the first grade are teetering on the brink of being left behind. Throw in a few negative societal influences; mix with a little social and cultural dysfunction, the natural confusion of adolescence and the label at risk becomes an understatement. As we have witnessed the unconscious destruction that many of these young men have perpetrated upon their own communities is there any question as to the importance of parental structure and balance. William Jenkins once stated, "Powerless people who have accepted their powerlessness as permanent have no desire to become educated, and education is their only avenue to freedom" (Jenkins).

I think about it often, and whenever I do I feel my muscles tighten. I can almost feel the anguish of all my people; that is to be physically bound and mentally shackled. Judging by the demeanor of many today one can almost understand just how easily slavery worked. I have to remind myself that we were a much stronger people at that time. Our people were beaten down with whips, chains, lies and lynching's. Mutilations were used as deterrents for those who would brave to run to their freedom. One would be killed or mutilated for trying to educate one's self or trying to stop the raping of one's woman or child. The mothers had to raise the man-child to be docile and to keep their heads down for fear of retaliation from an insecure or evil slave owner.

Today we are so soft. We are given so little yet we crave so much. Men who should be heads of households have turned their backs on their women and children; consequently we are a people in decline. We are the only people in history to have come out of bondage and not have moved forward to a better or higher social standing. Jewish people had a motto, "never forget," when referring to their holocaust. We as a people are guilty of not sharing the wisdom from one generation to the next, and so, we have forgotten. My decadent thrills theory: Good versus Evil; one demonstrates his or her ignorance and immaturity by their romance or enticement with things that God, mother, father, and the larger society has deemed inappropriate. Examples are as small as profanity and as large as criminality, and promiscuity of the many varieties. The older and educated individuals being just as suspect as the younger and ignorant, many are tantalized and tend to gravitate towards the negative.

My one in ten theory; we are so adept at following that many of us lose our own self identity. One of us will flourish, two will be alienated because of their success, and seven of ten will try to emulate the third. Five of us will resign or succumb to the ideal of materialism or oppressive stress. Three will manage to live well and two will have the opportunity to excel. One will advance forward and make a positive contribution to his people and therefore society. Recognized or not this contribution may be as small as just being the best parent he or she can be, or perhaps just a living example of proper conduct; which is living Godly. There will be those of that group of five that will try through their own ignorance or evil to tear down any and everything that the one has accomplished. Another sign that we have fallen short of God or even our own expectations is this constant need to be accepted or to belong. We have the expectation or need to be recognized and respected despite our personal failures. We need to understand that it is not so much in what one achieves, but how one goes about making that achievement.

One of us will flourish; two will be alienated because of their success, it is the unfortunate nature of a carnal man to be envious, man tries to wear one another down. Three of ten will try to emulate the third; should his success be wrought by unholy means the attraction will be even greater. Five of us will resign or succumb to the ideal of materialism and oppressive stress. Three will manage to live well and two will have the opportunity to excel. One will advance forward and make a positive contribution to God, his people, and therefore society.

Chapter Ten:
Lifespan Development & Personality

There are numerous aspects of human development, including physical, cognitive, social, moral, and personality development. Throughout a life time an individual will develop many different skill sets, beliefs, habits, and witness numerous physical changes. Plato and Aristotle had differing opinions on learning. Are humans born with certain innate knowledge and abilities, are they more influenced by the learning that occurs through the five senses. The most opportune time to influence a developing mind is childhood, 3-12 years of age. There are varying opinions on developmental psychology, nature versus nurture, continuity versus stages, and stability versus change. This is a very critical period in a lifetime; sensitivity to certain stimulus will shape an individual's future development. This influence will come from personal experience and from observation of others.

The integrationist perspective develops from an individual's personal predisposition and from experiences within the environment. Physical development or lack thereof is usually attributed to the interaction between the child and the father figure, with consideration given to health, heredity, and environment. Cognitive development is heavily affected by the mother; research shows the child's educational trail will reflect that of the mother. This age range borders on the early preoperational stage of development and includes the concrete and early formal operational stages of development (2008, Carpenter & Huffman).

The poet John Donne wrote, "No man is an island, entire of itself." Social development is explained by some using the imprinting or attachment theories. Just as the physicality of the youth is affected by the interaction with the father, the social development is greatly affected by the care giver. This can be the mother, father, or the baby sitter who all show high levels of affection and contact with the child.

This kind of stimulus is also referred to as contact comfort; the child in turn will manifest this nurturing as he or she grows in life.

Parents are and will continue to the best or the worst teachers when it comes to morality. One of the most influential researchers in moral development was Lawrence Kohlberg, who used several stages of development to make his point. The preconvention level; punishment and obedience orientation, conventional level, good child orientation (obey rules to get approval), or the social contract orientation (moral reasoning reflects belief in democratically accepted laws). Kohlberg believed these theories to be universal and invariant, and the age trends that are noticed tend to be rather broad, (Kohlberg, 1984).

The young adults who decided that they were not going to raise their children in the same fashion as their parents raised them have been major contributors to our downward spiral. They manifested what I called a reinforcement spanking into a total abusive beat down. I am sure some of these claims were legitimate; however many were the wails of spoiled and selfish individuals. They cultivated this story and nurtured it over time; it grew as they aged to the point until they believed it themselves. Consequently they abused their children by not taking the time to instill the proper moral and religious values that have sustained us for centuries.

This tendency of young, older and supposedly mature females to have children out of wedlock is another contributing factor. Make no mistake in many cases this is not happenstance of a promiscuous child; but rather planed outcome to prove the manhood of some confused young man. Also to garner attention for some affection starved female.

The families were all too eager to accept this illegitimate mind-set. There are a number of reasons why; like generational assisted living or just the fact that many have become familiar with taking the path of least resistance. It became too easy for the families and society to accept this crippling mentality rather than take some preventative measures. Educate your children if for no other reason to make them aware of what they're up against; give them a fighting chance, let that be your legacy.

Raise your children to be obedient but not oppressed; teach them to be cautious but not cowardly. Raise them to have faith, but not falsely, to be prepared, but not prejudiced, teach them to be confident, but not condescending. Above all; and this is very important, their education, must precede their emancipation. At this point in our history most Americans, Black, White, and other, by any other label you choose to place upon them; should be struggling to sleep.

There are a number of considerations one has as a result of population expansion. Will there be an availability of public services, such as housing and welfare? There is a misnomer as to which ethnicity dominates the welfare roles, most think of minorities. Single Caucasian females with children are in the majority of ethnic groups receiving public assistance. Medicare is a concern for the elderly, insurance for children and unemployed adults. Education attainment levels, individual marketability in a job market already pinched by the influx of emigration.

The new political catch phrases, "Global Economy," and "Out Sourcing," have caused a huge level of discontent from U.S. born citizens. Many believe we have become a consumer nation rather than a producing nation; with many jobs being outsourced to other countries. The situation with the Gulf War has not set well with the majority of Americans; it has put a strain on the country from an economic stand point.

The war budget has forced the government to cut back on many public services. Differing levels of desperation have produced some peculiar reactions. The crime rate is continuing to rise; burglary, armed robbery, assaults, drug dealing, and the homicide rates have reached record levels. Consequently many in Indianapolis and throughout our society have focused on the differences in one another. Not only that consideration; but this, the totality of the agenda of the republican and tea party is in ousting this president who happens to be a person of color.

Chapter Eleven:
Critical Thinking and Language

Language is the most primary and essential ingredient when it comes to basic communication. Conversation creates and stimulates the thought process. One of the reasons for much of the societal confusion and dysfunction we face today can be traced back to a failure to communicate. Society has decided any topic that is considered controversial will just simply not be discussed.

We have digressed so far that we have given it a name. "Politically Correct" is the catch phrase. The definition as far as many are concerned is, "to lie." If one individual or group is offended by a particular utterance it is deemed inappropriate for open dialog. Many things have changed in our society and many have gone unchanged by our refusal to have open conversation on some very controversial issues. Critical Thinking and Language; language plays a very important role in the critical thinking process. Speaking the same language would be one less barrier to over-come when working towards a particular point or goal. A diversity of tongues is of great benefit especially in this great melting pot we call America. Mental connection is vital when one is trying to persuade or sell a person or group on his or her product or point of view. Conversations in which you actively listen and show respect for the others opinion will make any thinking person want to hear and understand your reasoning. A reasonable and rational declaration will gain respect if not agreement; what you will have done is open the door for future discussions.

Language can empower and limit the expression of your thoughts in many ways, for example you must know to whom you are speaking. You do not want to intimidate or embarrass anyone, and you do not want to appear less than confident in your opinion. Some observation or prior knowledge of the person or persons to whom you will be engaging will eliminate any potential misunderstanding. Shared expression is advisable; as the comfort level raises so too will the level of engagement. General topics are safe, avoid assumptions, and know that many individuals are uncomfortable when discussing race, politics, religion, or preferences.

As for the role of critical thinking in persuasion the advantage lies with the swift thinking debater. We have all been made aware of phrases like the "gift of gab," or the "smooth talker." An individual with a ten word vocabulary would suffer in a verbal confrontation with one who thinks well on their feet.

Knowing how to turn a phrase separates the sellers from the buyers in most cases.

The spoken word can be a very instrumental tool, or a very deadly weapon. Words have escalated and de-escalated wars. Language has been used to lift individuals to another level of notoriety, and has been equally instrumental in their demise. Society has deemed those who are verbally challenged as less than intelligent, case and point "Ebonics." This broken English has roots more so in uneducated Southern Caucasians than the perceived inner city African American street slang. "Ebonics is perhaps most distinctive in its intonation and some stress patterns, which it still shares with white American Southern English in such instances as the stress in the word police falling on the first rather than the second syllable" (Encyclopedia Britannica).

Companionship plays a significant role in ones mental well being. In considering loneliness and solitude I must admit at this stage of life I had not given much thought to either. As stated in our reading, Corey and Corey emphasized the importance of distinguishing the difference between being alone and being lonely. There are times in life that one is confronted with circumstances beyond one's control. The death of my father triggered 20 years of constant moving. My family moved from Mississippi to Indiana, and once here we relocated annually. My siblings and I attended seven different elementary and middle schools, and two different high schools. Separation anxiety played a role as some of us were sent to live with an aunt and others to live with our grandmother. No one seemed to give any thought to the fact that we all witnessed the murder of our father.

My siblings and I definitely suffered from a lack of attachment and the shock of that incident would manifest itself later in all of our lives.

Solitude is something I have learned to savor. I am writing two books and I love to spend time browsing on the internet. I am not any longer a stranger to myself; I found God and learned to appreciate who I am and to accept the differences in those around me.

As for those who have not yet learned to confront the fear of loneliness I would suggest therapy. Some of us do create our own loneliness through shyness for a number of reasons; one being a low self image as was the case for many.

When considering loneliness and life stages my mind went back to the situation with my father; I have relived it enough times to have made it a building part of my mentoring talks with young children and adults. Adolescents and young adults have so many physical and psychological changes going on that poverty, relocation, and tragedy could be enough to push them over the edge. I pray that for every individual there is a period of inner peace prior to middle and advanced age as each of these stages brings on a plethora of physical and psychological life changes also.

I feel in many cases we have kicked our elderly to the curb in our endless pursuit of productivity, power, and attractiveness. In modern times we rush to the point of exhaustion and in that haste we make some bad decisions. Those were my thoughts as I read of the prevalence for divorce in our society. Divorce, depending upon the circumstances should be a last resort. It of no benefit to either of the involved parties, and I am sure affected their children in some very negative ways as well.

For individuals who have gone through this separation I hope they learn to see their time alone as a source of strength and a foundation for their relating to others. Perhaps they can find whatever they thought was missing in their relationship and have some reconciliation.

Considering death and loss; I see this as a trial of longevity. To be blessed with long life brings with it the reality you will witness the passing of many of those you love.

Many will ask the question of fulfillment; are you living the kind of life you wanted. I would hope that everyone feels they contributed to someone else in a positive way before their season here has expired. I could not imagine living a life in fear of death; however I am curious about those who choose not to believe in God. As I faced the deaths of my father, brother, sister, and many others I am not sure how it would have affected me if I had no faith. I believe culture has an affect on one's religious beliefs, culture and religion affects one's view on death and the meaning of life.

Suicide: as the ultimate choice, the ultimate surrender, or the ultimate tragedy? Suicide is one of the leading causes of death in the United States. The ultimate choice is the Lord, I believe if there was timely intervention or if this person could have somehow passed that particular moment he or she would have made a better decision. Someone would have had to be close enough to have noticed the symptoms; again I am guessing if they could have just passed that particular moment. I am a religious man, suicide is a sin, be it rational, assisted, or hastened death. What would my mindset be if I was in excruciating pain such as those who have requested ending their existence as an act of mercy?

Advance directives, freedom in dying, and the stages of death are considerations all should have in advance. I am sure for many, particularly the young this is something they would rather leave for a later time. I have had conversation with an individual who refused any concept of religion, or thought of dying until he was on his death bed.

His concern at that point was his own refusal to listen to advice from doctors and those who attempted to minister to him. He was remorseful and lamented over his lack of beliefs and opportunities he wasted. I found it interesting to read of how those who were facing death and those who were grieving over death, separation, or other losses experience similar responses. Culture again comes into play during the grieving process as many will not allow themselves to grieve.

The stages of denial, anger, bargaining, depression, and hopefully of acceptance are again visited. For the many who have not reconciled with the fact of death or significant loss, and isolate themselves, the reference of being dead psychologically, and socially applies to them. How well are you living life? The thought takes me back to early stages of my own story, the greatest tragedy for me would be, if, on my dying day, I would say that I didn't live my life, rather I lived someone else's life." I would consider that a tragedy indeed.

Let us take a moment to focus on our quest for identity, or the why of our existence. There are probably as many questions as there are influences on our personal makeup. We are acculturated first by our families, and then by different groups as we move through childhood, education, adulthood, employment, and differing life situations.

Hopefully one has developed religion or a positive set of core values or beliefs that influence how one conducts him or herself. In our search for meaning and purpose human beings are the only creature known who can reflect on their existence. Because of this men are primarily and essentially responsible for the direction they choose to go in life.

Victor Frankl defined logo therapy: "Everything can be taken from a man except one thing, the last of human freedoms; to choose one's attitude in any given set of circumstances" (Corey and Corey 2006).

Let's explore our pathways to personal growth and continued self exploration. The reading reemphasized Frankl's assertion that we control our personal actions and attitudes. I agree with the reading and writing programs as necessary for ongoing self assessment and if needed self directed behavioral changes. Support groups and counseling are excellent avenues toward self understanding for many of us. Dreams can also lead to self awareness as they tend to reveal significant aspects of our past and present struggles, as well as some joyful memories.

Through counseling and therapy one can explore the meaning of his or her dreams. In conclusion this course has lead to personal reflection; which like any good artist one needs to step back from his or her work to gain a better perspective.

Chapter Twelve:
Explorations in Personal Growth

Why do we behave as we do? If this is not the ultimate question it is certainly in the top five, there-in lies my curiosity. We seem to be very prone to follow group thinking, but we profess loudly our personal uniqueness. Ultimately the majority of us conform to the prevailing societal norm of our time period. The question, "what is social psychology?" will be answered in many diverse ways depending upon whom you ask.

The examples in the introduction were compelling. When you think of the situations and circumstances that occurred at Jones Town, Columbine, or Heaven's Gate, our curiosity is peaked with each incident. From the bombardment of opinion from media, to their analysis on the latest hypothesis of professional psychoanalyst, the end result remains the same. Ultimately we are left pondering the eternal question, why?

Our acculturation is evidenced by the power of social interpretation; we want so badly to fit in that we abandon to a degree the concept of self. The definition of construal is the way in which people perceive, comprehend, and interpret the social world. We work so hard at conformity in our youth that many never escape from this social mind meld. It is truly the unique individuals who are able to self actualize; the remainder of us are left in admiration of their achievements.

There is no perfect science when doing research on social psychology. We must have a good historical record but keep in mind that these hypotheses were based mainly on personal observations. The "limits of the correlation method" for example; correlation does not equal causation. Researchers measure the influence of the independent and dependent variables in an attempt to ascertain reasonably sound hypotheses, which in reality could be more influenced by an unknown variable.

Many researchers base their conclusions on what they call cross cultural research. I assume the thought process here is to test as many samples as possible and then compare commonalities; close but probably not pure science. Ultimately we are left with the fact that one's most compelling influence will come from his or her immediate environment. Their belief system will be influenced primarily and profoundly by their family, and the interaction between the child and the parents, or the lack there of. Their social psychology or behavioral tendencies will be formed by the combination of these variables.

How do we think about the social world? When I read the stories of Amadou Diallo, Timothy Thomas, and Tamir Rice my first thought was of just how many times this has happened in our society. As I read of low effort thinking I flashed back to an episode I witnessed at a local high school. A young student upon hearing news of a shocking event turned to her father and asked if he thought this event was true; he turned to her with confidence and stated that it must be true, "it was on television!" I then thought about just how programmable many of us really are.

I thought about slavery, the holocaust, and ethnic cleansing, all horrific crimes against humanity, and at that moment I could almost understand how persuasive some mindsets can be. These mentalities of self fulfilling prophecies have left us with some serious consequences. Racism is alive and well in these United States simply because we refuse to let go of the representativeness heuristic.

Politicians and business persons alike will focus on our ethnicities to make the point that I am like you and they are not. Race baiting has been a separation tactic used by many to take our concentration away from the reality of the issues. In the case of a United States senator who would be president, the attention was navigated away from reality and focused on his name.

Many, with very little reflection, were convinced that he must be a terrorist; his name is Barack Obama. The power of suggestion or a persuasive argument by an individual, who has garnered much respect, can convince the masses of almost anything. With that thought my mind flashed back to the Jonestown and Heaven's Gate tragedies. You don't have to convince them all, just enough to influence some to go out socially and speak on your behalf.

When considering social perception we have become increasingly more sensitive about how we are perceived in our living environment. We are aware of every nonverbal form of communication and we actually look for signs of disagreement or agreement. Many of us watch intently the facial and body expressions of everyone we are engaged in some form of communications with. Many tend to have self serving attributions as defense mechanisms to salvage their fragile self esteem. A great man, who had his critics as we all do, went on to become president of the United States. He stated that we should not stand in judgment of any people; "for they are just what we would be, under similar circumstances." His name was Abraham Lincoln.

A passage in the Holy Bible, Romans: chapter 12, verse 2, states; "be you not conformed to this world, 'but be ye transformed by the renewing of your mind." God's children who are afraid to be different from the world around them will lose the power of their testimony to God. Someone once told me that the only time it was cool to be just like everyone else was in middle school. I wish the previous statement were true; however, this belonging need seems to follow many of us all of our lives.

Prosperity or level of educational attainment notwithstanding, many have this inert need to belong with a group of like thinkers. In our reading the informational social influence or the need to know what is right is a powerful motivator. What is right or wrong for many may seem obvious but for some it depends on their desire or perhaps some prevailing social motivation.

Abortion for example has united people on both sides of the issue. I want to believe that the vast majority of people would not condone the taking of life at any stage. At the same time how can anyone tell a female that she has to carry a baby full term regardless of the circumstances. The argument continues as the orphanages and the foster homes fill to capacity; unfortunately, with all of these well intentioned mindsets there are plenty of empty seats at the adoption agencies.

Group thinking has been a bane on our society, preceding slavery, civil rights, and the feminist movements. As we arrive in the 21st century bigotry continues to claw at our reasoning as we let levels of

income, education, immigration, and class join with all
the other negative motivations that segregate our
society.   I particularly enjoyed the reading on how
deindividuation makes people feel less accountable.
The example of Harper Lee's novel "To Kill a
Mockingbird," was a perfect lesson point.   When
Scout succeeded in reminding them of their humanity,
the mob mentality was broken down to a collection of
responsible citizens.   Scout was obviously one of the
rare individuals who self actualized and conformity
was not in her genetic makeup.

Speaking   of   one's   genetic   makeup   and
interpersonal attraction, how does one define love?
There are so many intangibles in the life of every
individual.   When one is asked to define love, it's
more commonly preceded with a pause.   Then they
query with a series of open ended questions such as
family influence and family love.   They ask if this is a
friendship love, romantic love, or if this is a search for
a mate.   After all of that confusion, consideration
must be given to cultural and societal influences on
the individual's expectations when choosing a mate.
Many find it simpler just to have sex and eliminate the
confusion; consequently, they made commitments
that they were unaware of and they find the confusion
has only begun.

Love has a great deal to do with assimilation, this
is not global warming but the title of making a
difference in social psychology, and attaining a

111

sustainable future reminded me of this underrated social dilemma. When one studies the fatherless rates, the education and crime rates the correlation should be obvious. A wise old philosopher once said, "A society that leaves the responsibility of raising the male child to the mother is a society on a road to destruction." Where is the love? This "pro-social behavioral" concern needs to be addressed and given a very high priority, as we are already behind in the cause and effect that it is having on our communities. Children, who live absent their biological fathers, on average, are more likely to fall subject to the stereotype threat, to be poor, experience educational, health, emotional and psychological problems.

They are more likely to be victims' of child abuse and engage in criminal behavior than their peers who live with their married biological mother and father.

While assessing the effectiveness of intervention associations such as the C.I.S.D. (Critical Incident Stress & Debriefing), I believe such organizations are needed to study the psychological effects of traumatic events such as multiple deaths within our American communities.

Early intervention into the lives of both dysfunctional children and parents is needed to stop this downward spiral. For a child, failing academically as early as the third grade should be a warning to both parents, educators, and the greater society that more attention is needed. As for parents who are young or ignorant as to what their responsibilities require of them, there are resources available to them.

As for resolving social dilemmas for example, through collaboration, the federal government and corporate America have established "School to Work," programs. Many companies,' unfortunately not enough, have established partnerships with community schools in what is called "Adopt a School Programs," whereby the employees are assigned a student to mentor. This is a kind of job shadowing program.

The youth are introduced to a variety of positive life experiences while they learn the responsibilities and expectations that come with the daily adult work routine. Father programs such as "Security Dads," were or have been established and set up in schools, churches and community centers to provide mentors to, "not only the youth," but to other mothers, fathers, young and older adults in need of proper life models as well. Organizations that understand the need to intervene early also understand the necessity of having the parent, guardian or mentor involved in this proactive effort to salvage the state of our youth. In other words they are using social psychology to achieve a sustainable future. One could say that these corporations are supplying some needed love.

My initial consideration to this writing assignment was one of personal reflection. In 1998 vice president

Al Gore and his wife Tipper co-authored a book titled "Joined at the Heart." A chapter in the book "resilience" was dedicated to me and chronicled the many life changing events that shaped me into the person I am today.

My wife, a friend and associate Dr. Jackie Greenwood, and I were flown to Washington D.C. to spend a week at the white house with then sitting president and first lady Bill and Hillary Clinton. We spent the week sharing with the president, vice president, first and second ladies our theories on racism, poverty, the breakdown of the family structure, fathering deprivation, single parent homes, and the effect these realities were having on the educational attainment or lack thereof, of many of our country's youth, and the subsequent adverse effect on our society.

When considering social psychology and the law, I thought of just how programmed and biased many of the individuals were that I have encountered in my life. It is a constitutional right to be judged by a jury of one's peers; however, there are those within ethnic groups that are very prejudicial against those of their own ethnicity. We are a society that has accepted many of the stereotypical beliefs as reality. Eyewitness accounts are subject to what is defined as the false memory syndrome. I thought of the movie "12 Angry Men" and another classic that we discussed previously in class, "To Kill a Mocking

Bird." In recent memory the O.J. Simpson trial or the verdicts reached in the many police action shootings; one example being the Amadou Diallo shooting.

How does one explain personality? There is no exact science when studying human emotion or motivation. The definition of theory was well placed at the beginning of this offering. I found myself revisiting the description of both theory and personality as I moved forward in my reading. There are so many influences upon one's personality, and reactions to a similar stimulus are common to very diverse. Upon reading we found that basic philosophical assumptions are evidence to my statement; there is no exact art. The basic philosophical assumptions of personality are basically individual assumptions.

There is not a specific value or provable piece of evidence that cannot be scrutinized or viewed from a differing perspective by another studying the same case. From the macro and micro theories to the academic and clinical approaches, I believe that the conclusions will ultimately leave you with a question.

Verifiability is a statement of scientific authenticity, that is the study and the theory behind it must be verifiable. Based upon intense study the ideology has to specify how it can be proven or disproven. Falsification as defined in our text states that scientific statements must be open to falsification.

The researcher or scientist must point out the circumstance in which his or her conclusions may be proven to be untrue. I loved this quote from our reading, "Science is an offspring of philosophy and its' methods are the fruit of philosophy's labors. The methods of art, science, and philosophy are distinguishable but not unrelated; they complement one another and together provide us with a fuller understanding." I found myself contemplating more than writing when considering Freud's theories on the Id, Ego, and Super ego. The Id as Freud describes is the core of our being. This is our basic and most self appeasing primitive drive, in the German translation "Es hunger mich." Freud uses the pleasure principle and the wish fulfillment principle to emphasize his point.

The Ego works to satisfy all the selfish desires of the Id. The Ego utilizes the reality principle and thrives to quench the hunger of the Id by moral and acceptable means. This reaction is dependent upon the rearing and cultural environment of the child. All things being proper and in order the secondary processes have been developed enough to elicit a humane response.

The Super Ego is the direct outcome of parental preparation, a value system, a moral standing, and a conscience. Freud points out that this is integral to self evaluation and the cultivation of an ego-ideal. Our society has produced some startling attitudes in both young and supposedly mature individuals. One only has to look at the state of our economy, our crime, and poverty rates to see this self first mindset is truly a detriment to our societal well being.

I read with interest Freud's theories on the psychosexual stages of development, my question on the Oral stage was, "is this truly a psychosexual stage"? As humans we are born practically helpless. At this stage of development the only thing one has control of is their mouth. Our only instinct is to feed; consequently everything is directed to our mouths. Anal, and I hate the term anal retentive. I am not qualified to question a gentleman the likes of Freud, however, could this be a case of over thinking. I can understand a child being stimulated as a parent gently cleans their genital area, and perhaps this does begin awareness in the memory of the child. The memory is manifested more so in later stages as the stimulation continues. Freud referred to the two primary modes of anal expression as retention, expulsion, and he went on to explain how they contributed to future character traits.

Abraham Maslow as declared by some the spiritual father of humanistic psychology was on target with his theory on human motivation. I could relate to his humble if not dysfunctional family beginnings. As a child of immigrants he faced a great deal of discrimination in his youth. I am sure his environment had a great deal to do with his evolution into humanistic psychology. Maslow's hierarchy of needs is a perfect learning tool for all studying in this field. I believe that to understand the motivation of others one has to have a firm grasp on the understanding of one's self. I was equally enthused by Carl Rodgers and his theory of personality. The self concept is an area of study I feel each individual needs to delve into. I believe many, if not most, of our concerns about society could be remedied if we just had a better grasp of our own personality makeup.

I studied psychology and sociology in high school. I do recall my instructor, Mr. Oglesby, who always brought very enlightening dialog. Now given that I have had time to think about it, that's exactly why I liked the class. Mr. Oglesby took the time, as an educator, to open up to each student and encourage them in a unique way. May God rest my friend Mr. Oglesby's soul! I now realize that I learned quite a bit from him and why I enjoyed the inclusive class demeanor. Freud stated that the goal of therapy was to make the unconscious conscious. He certainly made that the goal of his work as a theorist. This was the beginning, and many followed in his footsteps, many gave him credit, many did not. The differences in personality theorists like George Kelly, Albert Ellis, Aaron Beck, Francis Cecil Sumner, and Arnold Lazarus can be attributed to fundamental differences in philosophical assumptions.

Random thought; I understand from the research of this generation's preoccupation with sex, I was lead to believe "together with the work of Alfred Kinsey, Bertrand Russell, and others he instigated the social – sex revolution of the 1960s." Ellis's A-B-C theory of personality underlying rational emotive behavior was interesting reading; however, I would like to read of his opinion on Freud's psychosexual stages of personality.

I have always been concerned about the mental conditioning of many of the individuals I have encountered. In reading of the focus on types of conditioning and behavior modification gave me a better understanding of some of the radical viewpoints I have witnessed.

I have noticed a great number of individuals performing at a very basic level. For example the drive, cue, response, and reinforcement learning basically can be compared to Freud's Id; minus the Ego or Super Ego. I am also a true believer in the observational learning theory. All one has to do is pay attention to many uneducated adults and confused teen agers. There is an old saying that if no contradictory evidence is given many will believe whatever they receive. I have witnessed many a woman and man throw their lives away, and do so with enthusiasm. Many are reluctant to standout on their own and compromise themselves in their attempts to assimilate into certain social groups.

Cloud Of Dust

Allport's definitions of maturity should be required reading for the many who claim adulthood; or the ever popular immature statement, "I'm grown!" We are all unique individuals in our own right, but share many common traits. I believe this fact terrorizes many of us who would prefer that no one was aware of our personal dispositions.

Surface traits and source traits are the building blocks of personality according to Cattell. Source traits are the underlying variables that all psychologists strive to uncover. Cattell's influence on the big five personality traits is just another example of the evolution of psycho analogy that began with Freud. I find it hard to accept that many of these individuals; Eysenck for example, was very critical of his predecessors in their chosen field of expertise. The evolution seemed quite natural to me; someone had a vision, and others expanded on that vision. I do hope the exploration continues, as of today many are totally unaware of their personal selves. Maybe once we get this self think thing figured out we will in the words of Rodney King, "Why can't we all just get along!"

Finally we must consider the holistic nature of developmental psychology, the two major dimensions of parenting, permissiveness and restrictiveness, and the multitude of variables that fall within these definitions. I believe Freud's latency stage is a place to draw the line in developmental psychology. The childhood developmental stage from 6 to 12 years of age is Freud's latency period; Erikson's industry versus inferiority stage and Piaget's concrete operational stage. At this life stage the child will acquire and use cognitive operations as they haven't prior to this point. The mental components that are necessary for logical thought will be manifested at this stage of life. Proper nurturing, and depending on prior stimulation or influence, intervention is needed at this stage.

Behavioral patterns set at this time will have a major effect on the future of the child. Failing grades as early, as the second or third grades, should give both parents and educators the realization that more intervention is needed. This is not to say that the preceding stages are any less vital than the latency stage; however, our goals are made all the more difficult if the preceding stages were dysfunctional. My point is that intervention at this stage is crucial under normal conditions, but is extremely important for the proper developmental behaviors to be cultivated should some percentage of nurturing have been by-passed previously.

There is in my opinion no excuse for apathetic or uninvolved parenting, teen pregnancies, births out of wedlock, and fatherlessness notwithstanding. These numbers however have been skewed and used to distract from the reality of the embedded big business and politician relationships. Poverty is a major contributor to all the prior mentioned afflictions. Our business and political leadership in their infinite wisdom has decided that a global economy is beneficial to not only the United States but for all industrialized nations as well. The subsequent outsourcing has all but wiped out the American middle class and greatly increased the poverty level.

Poverty has proven to have a detrimental effect on patriotism and parenting alike. This is evidenced by the breakdown of the family structure and the patriotic dissention exhibited by many American citizens. Why would another government want to deal with a nation of leaders who are not loyal to their own citizenry? Perhaps our internal turmoil and dissention is a motivator for them; or perhaps it is just the power of the almighty dollar.

Chapter Thirteen:
American Revolutionary Significance

In answer to the preponderance of queries as to why a people; or any people for that matter act as they do, I am compelled to share with you my "Octal-theorem." There are many antecedents to human behavior; however, we cannot explore them all in this writing. We will set eight as a limiting figure, which should be sufficient enough to provide any person of average reasoning ability with not only clarity, but a profound understanding of the initial query. In my studies of Indiana history I found that many base the significance of the American Revolution on the State of Indiana as Thomas Jefferson's establishment of the Northwest Ordinance. Just as significant was a mindset of superiority that was allowed to prevail and manifest itself in the psyche of this newly forming union. Of the myriad of profound literary statements observed within the context of my learning experience the following quote gave me pause. According to Ralph D. Gray, "admitting for the moment that the political civilization of the United States may in the distant future be submerged beneath communism, fascism, race worship, technocracy, or whatever fashions in government that the future may bring forth, the fact remains that very often time permits political ideals to outlive the death of the civilization that produces them."

We have not seen the end of our current civilization; however, one has to consider the countries legacy were it to have fallen under Spanish, French, or a continuation under British rule. The conquest of the Northwest Territory not only established the land boundaries that would include the state Indiana but also led to the legislation that is considered to be the greatest piece of written and agreed upon legislation second only to the Constitution of the United States of America. Gray referred to this compact as "the true origin of all free government, a free and unforced covenant or agreement, the highest and most sacred sanction for political power known to man." The establishment of the Northwest Ordinance was a watershed for the fledgling United States as a country; however, early in historic times, Native Americans pressured by the Spanish, French, British, Americans, and other Indian allies, were forced out of central Wisconsin, into Southwestern Wisconsin, Northwestern Illinois, and Northeastern Iowa. Many settled near the rapids of the Mississippi river, an area known today as Keokuk, Iowa. Some settled near the Rock River in Illinois, and along the Osage and Missouri Rivers in the late

1700s. In 1804, Indian leaders signed what would prove to be a disastrous treaty. By its terms they forfeited all of their land in the area of the Mississippi River in both Illinois and Iowa. Most of the Native American people were outraged.

The Tribes were then in Iowa, after having been forced west by the Americans. These settlers continued to push and wanted more land. In 1828, President John Adams without notice had the Indian lands in Iowa sold. The Indians returned from their winter hunt during that period and found that their lands had been purchased. Abraham Lincoln and Jefferson Davis, President of the Confederate States of America, fought against the Indians in what was called the Blackhawk war. President, Zachary Taylor, waged war against these Native Americans as well. Long after Lincoln inked the Emancipation Proclamation, up and through the recent Civil rights era, we find ourselves still mired in a racially tense environment. Americans arrived in this country to escape the tyranny of their English ancestors, only to reinvent the pretentious superior mindset they were attempting to escape from.

Professor Bernard Sheehan argues that perhaps it is possible that the label of savages and charges of inhumanity and cruelty were laid at the wrong door.

Gray spent many moments in contemplation of the British after acquiring the Illinois country sans the signage of the Treaty of Paris. This was vast area of the country previously controlled by the French. The British proclamation of 1763 was to discourage any settlement of this country until the Indian title to the land had been extinguished. They were slowed in this take over by the limited success of an Indian uprising famously known as Pontiac's Rebellion. This was referred to as an uprising; natives fighting for survival in their own homeland usurping both French and British control during the Indian war of 1763-1765.

George Rogers Clark and Lieutenant Governor Henry Hamilton collided in their efforts for conquest and had many commonalities in their dealings with Native Americans. Many historians now question the impact of their signing of the peace settlement of 1783.

The fallacy of both Hamilton and Clark was in their use and treatment of the Indians; consequently, their conflict would touch on the deepest strains of American commitment during its revolutionary trial. Hamilton's reputation was of manipulating the Indians to perform horrific acts, he was known as the hair buyer for purchasing the scalps of the enemy soldiers from the Indians. Clark was known for his imitating of Indian war tactics and encouraging his troops to practice barbaric warfare. Clark often criticized the Indians stating when communicating one must maintain a simple vocabulary suitable for a primitive people…sound familiar?

This was the opinion of a man who had no formal education himself. One would assume that had he tried communicating in their native language, he would witness a much smoother dialog. Hamilton for his contributions to this mindset symbolized the conflict as a battle between liberty and tyranny, and between civilization and savagery. Gray in a summation of both personalities stated in the defense of civility they became savages.

In 1785 the consideration of statehood brought with it this stipulation, the population must exceed 60,000 people in general, but only 5,000 voters. These 5,000 voters must be adult white males. The Northwest Ordinance did however contain the precedent setting prohibition of slavery in the Northwest Territory. This is but one legacy of the American Revolution on the State of Indiana. Thomas Jefferson's establishment of the Northwest Ordinance was indeed a crowning moment in the history of these United States. Again one must give consideration to the prevailing mindset of superiority that followed the first settlers from their mother England. As for the contemplation Gray placed on the civilization of the United States and the distant future being submerged beneath a particular form of government or a prevailing mindset, the fact remains that we as a country have not lived up to the political ideals set forth in the Northwest Ordinance, or the constitution of the United States of America. We have not seen the end of our current civilization; however, one has to consider the countries legacy were it ever to have a true and open dialog covering the abolishment of any form of discrimination. Was this the greatest piece of written and agreed upon legislation second only to the Constitution of the United States of America? Mr. Gray referred to this compact as "the true origin of all free government, a free and unforced covenant or agreement, the highest and most sacred sanction for political power known to man."

Contrary to the opinion of Mr. Meredith Nicholson, and many other prominent writers of Indiana history; unless one is of celebrity, they will find the myth of Hoosier hospitality to be just that, "mythical." Ethnicity aside, there seems to be a prevailing mindset on what many believe is a minority of Indianapolis and Indiana residents. The history of the Negro in the state of Indiana, ostensibly a free state, was at best an insecure one. Emma Lou Thornbrough wrote of some unfortunate yet educationally enlightening episodes in Indiana history.

Another piece of unfortunate Indiana history is the Ku Klux Klan. Many people have an historic image of the Ku Klux Klan permanently etched in their minds. Men, dressed in white robes and hoods, riding throughout the countryside harassing the Negro. Many want to believe that the KKK is an extinct organization, once comprised of rednecks and racist southerners. However; and unfortunately, the Klan mentality is still alive and well in this country and prejudice has for many become institutionalized. How is it then that this terroristic hate group is allowed to thrive in a nation that has written hate crime legislation into law? To refer to this as freedom of speech is a contradiction to the intent of the legislation. This mentality is no longer the province of the angry Caucasian male. Hatred being an equal opportunity discriminator has become for many a separation of classes and like causes. "Ethnicity included!"

Chapter Fourteen:
Life in the Capital City

The founding fathers appreciated their opportunity and labored from the beginning in the interest of morality and enlightenment. Nicholson referred to Indianapolis as a city comparable to Jerusalem; "a city at unity with itself." A place where the tribes assemble; and where the seat of judgment is established, it is in every sense the capital of all the Hoosiers. Exactly what the definition of Hoosier is depends upon who you ask, and at what point in history one finds themselves. The history of the Negro in the state of Indiana, which at the time was considered to be a free state, was at best an insecure one. Emma Lou Thornbrough chronicles the history of slavery in the state and the mindset of many such as the Quakers who opposed the practice. Professor Thornbrough wrote of the very suspect Fugitive Slave Law In Operation. The story of John Freeman of Indianapolis gave light to a mentality that has flourished up until contemporary time.

Nicholson spoke of the many ethnic groups that passed through yet did not settle in Indiana, one would assume that it was more than just the view that discouraged them. He also made mention of the quantity of Negro voters in early Indiana history and that Indianapolis in particular is known for the stability of its population. Indianapolis is known as a city that is distinguished primarily by the essentially American character of its' people. Thomas Hamilton spoke of the hurrying about in pursuit of wealth; how this trait leads to immorality, which contributed to this decease of selfishness. Perhaps this is the manifestation of our English heritage that sailed over with the first settlers.

Hamilton went on to describe **American character** as the obsession with business and wealth. The American preoccupation with money cuts across all regional and class lines, and inevitably leads to dishonesty. Thomas Hamilton goes so far as to contend that Americans chose the dollar sign over the cross. "Whenever his love of money comes in competition with his zeal for religion, the latter is sure to give way. The whole race of Yankee peddlers is proverbial for dishonesty." Now that is the opinion of one individual, as is the case of any historical offering. Nicholson spoke well of the city founders with words such as faith, courage, and hardihood. He noted that too great a stress cannot be laid on their work. They sacrificed their personal ambition for the good of the community. That is a mindset to be admired; however, curiosity compels the question, were the founders concerned about the well being of the entire community, or just the necessary 5000 voting Caucasian males.

Indianapolis is well known as a town that does not except change very well, the writer assumes that this mindset can be attributed back to the religious prejudices of the early settlers. Indiana history will continue to be chronicled positively, in particular by sentimental Hoosier scribes. Hoosier hospitality may prove to be just that; a people of simple domesticity, as the writer described them; home loving, and home keeping. The history of the Negro in the state of Indiana will for some time conjure up memories of the Ku Klux Klan. Many people have this image of the Ku Klux Klan permanently etched in their minds.

Meredith Nicholson stated that Indianapolis is still considered a town that became a city against its will! The residents liked their slow way; however, when the situation could no longer be avoided Hoosiers creased their trousers, shined their shoes and accepted evolution with good grace. That being said; there is something neighborly and cozy about Indianapolis.

A revolution by any other name; *A revolution as defined by Sociology*, a radical and pervasive change in society and the social structure, especially one made suddenly and often accompanied by violence. Giving all due respect to Mr. James Madison, and also to any other individual who may disagree. Regardless of station, place, or impact upon a particular individual; the fact that there was no actual physical war does not demean the fact that there was resistance to a shift in society. There have been numerous incidents since Indiana received its statehood that fall into the category of a revolutionary resistance. There were Indian uprisings that continued after statehood; this was a people fighting the controlling powers for survival in their home land. John Freeman and the condition of slavery at that time was a revolution in affect. The rise of the Klu Klux Klan considering the numbers involved and the lasting mental legacy was and still is revolutionary. In contemporary times the attitudes towards big business and politics and what many believe is that higher education is unattainable for them; and consequently is a barrier placed between them and acquiring the American dream. Revolutions of the mind actual or perceived are in the mind of the beholder; therefore, actual or perceived, one's perception is one's reality.

Cloud Of Dust

The dean of Indiana historians, Mr. James Madison, contended that in the history of the state of Indiana there have been no revolutions. A revolution by any other name is still a revolution. Were it not for the fact that the American Indians were considered savage and less than human they would have been considered revolutionary in their fight to maintain their home land. According to Dale Benington, "This area of the three rivers was a site of settlement for Native Americans for as much as 10,000 years." The collection of villages known as Kekionga, located in the present day lakeside neighborhood, was a center of the Miami nation in historic times. Kekionga was also the gathering place for the Huron, the Ottawa, and the Shawnee. Kekionga; by traditional translation means "the blackberry patch." The Miami considered this an ancient sacred place. Benington described Kekionga in the 1790's as being a very large settlement called "Miami Town" by eastern Americans who feared the place as the center of Indian resistance to the expanding United States frontier.

Another counterpoint to Mr. Madison's assertion is the legacy of John Freeman, a free African American, seized in Indianapolis, and claimed to be the property of a gentleman by the name of Pleasant Ellington, who was a Methodist from the state of Missouri. Freeman himself would have to prove that he was not the person he was alleged to be. The United States Marshal consented to this provided that he would go to jail, and pay three dollars a day for a guard to keep him secure! Secure being the operative word as many would confiscate or kill runaway slaves at this time in history. Slavery was a condition that led to the Civil war, and was also a continuation of the mentality that manifested itself from the earliest settler to modern times. This mindset led to the Civil Rights movement and is a continual plaque upon the American psyche; the battle against this discrimination is revolutionary.

The golden age of agriculture brought with it another form of revolution; the industrialization of our nation and the subsequent rise of big business. Historian Rickie Lazzerini believes that along with the rise of big business came corruption. Bankers and corporate leaders became bedfellows with the politicians creating a bond that resulted in business-friendly laws. From these mergers, came monopolies that put a strain on the working citizens and communities of the state. Lazzerini commented on what was called the political bosses of the state such as Oliver P. Morton and Daniel Voorhees who used questionable tactics to influence political elections. These illegal activities unfortunately were not uncommon during the late 19th century. According to Lazzerini, unionism and grange movements were backlashes to big business practices which led to the reform movement of the early 20th century.

Blogs on the website motherjones.com are testimonies of the powerlessness felt by many, not just in the state of Indiana, but nationwide. Politicians don't care as one writer put it; "people don't know what to do with the anger they have," "they feel blocked by the senators and representatives." "Many believe there is a layer between Americans and the villains on Wall Street, and that is congress!" "Fear not loathing has set in as the public believes that any attack on Wall Street would leave the public fighting for rat meat on the streets." We all are a part of America and we cannot claim to be exempt, just because the war is not fought on your land does not provide for you a shelter from the consequences of the fallout, this is revolutionary.

Again, a revolution as defined by sociology as a radical and pervasive change in society and the social structure. We have given respect to Mr. James Madison, and also to any other individual who may disagree. Regardless of antecedent, behavior, or consequence thereof upon a particular individual; the fact that there was no actual physical war fought on your land does not demean the fact that there was resistance to a shift in our society. The reference was made to the numerous incidents since Indiana received its statehood that fall into the category of a revolutionary resistance. The battles once referred to as Indian uprisings that continued after statehood were in this writer's opinion revolutionary. This was a people fighting the controlling powers for survival in their home land just as any American citizen would consider the battle for our independence. John Freeman's battle for freedom which was personal to him at that time yet brought light to a condition of slavery that was a revolution in waiting. The rise of the Klu Klux Klan considering the numbers involved and the lasting mental legacy was and still is revolutionary. In contemporary times the attitudes towards big business and politics and what many believe is that equality of employment and education is unattainable for them. Many believe a barrier is placed between them and acquiring the American dream. Revolutions of the mind actual or perceived are in the mind of the beholder; therefore, actual or perceived one's perception is one's reality. Why do they act as they do? The dust is yet to settle!

Cloud Of Dust

These Words,

My Lord is writing all the time...

These words gather up in number resembling the fowl flying south, these words billow like thunder in my mind yet not my mouth, For God controls these words. In our heart these words begin the trust to reveal Gods truth that lies within us, through these words one can expound via conjugated verb or expressive noun.

These words I cannot bind reside in the hemispheres of my mind I can't hide the suppression of the souls decried so I deliver unto you the vestige of Gods blessed message, a respite for contemplative pause...

With Gods words we heed the call of the few that are chosen not the multitude that fall. These words of confession we pray atone for the poisonous seeds we each have sown, when in revelation the trumpet sounds we pray at last these words resound, well done in my soul consideration, yet not depart from me in full wrath of Gods frustration...We Must Heed These Words....

My Lord is writing all the time, and I just can't thank him enough.

"What will be the state of humankind when the dust finally settles?"

Security DAD Inc.

F. A. T. H. E. R.

Pastor Anthony D. Wallace I

About the Author

Reverend Pastor Anthony D. Wallace I - is simply a sinner who has been saved by grace and is a dedicated servant of our Lord and Savior Jesus Christ. Reverend A. D. Wallace I - is by Education, MA Ministry, Child Youth & Family Psychology, with 35 years of mentoring to the fatherless and the needy and educated in Christian life experience is capable of rendering Mediation and Reconciliation Services. On December 21, 2008, Reverend Anthony D. Wallace was called by God as a Minister of the gospel of Jesus Christ, Co-Founding New Spiritual Life Christian Church on March 3, 2012 with the theme, "*And* I will give you pastors according to mine heart, which shall feed you with knowledge and understanding." **(Jeremiah 3:11-15)**

Background - Pastor Anthony D. Wallace I

A.D. Wallace was born on August 4, 1954 in Hernando, Mississippi; he attended I.P.S. Arsenal Technical, & Arlington High School, Graduating in 1973. Rev. Wallace is the Pastor of New Spiritual Life Christian Church. He attended the University of Indianapolis, Bachelor Liberal Studies, Minor in Psychology, Indiana Wesleyan University @ Merion,

Wesley Seminary MA Ministry, Child, Youth & Family Psychology. Reverend Wallace has over 30 years experience mentoring the fatherless and the needy. He is Co Founder & Pastor of New Spiritual Life Christian Church; He is Co Founder & Chief Visionary Officer of the Father's Alliance Security Dad's Inc. Fatherhood & Family Consultant for MiddWall Consulting LLC, Indiana State Parents & Teachers Association, and Fatherhood & Family Consultant for U.I.T.E. (Urban Institute of Training & Education). Reverend Wallace is happily married to Linda Ann Cheney-Wallace for 43 years and they have been blessed with 2 Children: Anthony II, (wife: Venus), Lena L. (husband: Eric L. Middleton), and 8 Grandchildren: Latrice, Anthony III & Anthony IV, Toni, Nattily, Austin, Erica, & Lawrence, 1Great grandchild Christopher.

Rev. A.D. Wallace I and his siblings witnessed the murder of their father, and five of seven survived the potentially devastating after effects. This rendering of letters is biographic to a point, we hope enlightening in its teaching, and I pray interesting in its concept as a novel.

1989: The birth of the Security Dads Program.

➤ **1992:** Featured in Parade Magazine and the Indianapolis Star

➤ **1993:** The Indianapolis Education Association Human Rights Award.

➤ **1994:** Martin Luther King Drum Major Award; Featured on Good Morning America, Cable News Network (CNN), Discovery Channel, and various local channels (ABC, CBS, NBC, FOX, WTTV, the Recorder On Air Report, and the IPS Educational Channel); Featured in the New York Times, Red Book, Good Housekeeping, Jet, News Week, Ebony, Men's Health, The Futurist, and local Newspapers...

➤ **1994:** Founders of United Water, Arlington H.S. Adopt a School Internship Program.

➤ **1995:** Proclamation of Security Dads Day by Governor Evan Bayh, May 8, 1995; National Governor's Associations Distinguished Service Award; 109th Indiana General Assembly (House Concurrent Resolution No. 65) Proclamation; Governors Exemplary Project Award.

➤ **1996:** Honorary Guest and Honorary Mention in Governor Evan Bayh's State of the State Address; Mayors Volunteer

Partnership Award; Stone on the Canal Walk.

➤ **1997:** The Indianapolis Education Association Human Rights Award.

➤ **1998:** Vice President came to visit Security Dads at Arlington High School; White House Conference on School Safety in Washington D.C., special guest of Vice President Al Gore, Honorable Mention by President Bill Clinton.

➤ **1999 – 2002:** Members of the Expert Forum and Stage Presenters for Family Reunion Conference in Nashville, TN, moderated by Vice President Al Gore; Father of Distinction Award by the Circle City chapter of Links; Visited by High School Principals from Nova High School in Moscow Russia; Mayors Character Counts Award; Today show with Al & Tipper Gore; Featured in book "Joined at the Heart" authored by Al and Tipper Gore; Featured in book "From Father to Son" authored by Evan Bayh; Presenters at numerous fathers conferences nationally.

➤ **2004:** Mayors Community Service Award, Stone on the Canal Walk

➤ **2006:** Phillips Temple Church Martin Luther King Community Service Recognition.

➤ Greater St. Mark Church

Community Service Recognition.

➤ United Water Indiana Community Spirit Recognition.

➤ United Water National Care to Share Award.

➤ **2007:** Indiana Pacers Sports & Entertainment "Indiana Heroes" Recognition, Stacy Toran Foundation Community Service Recognition, "Inaugural DADS Inc. Fatherhood Hall of Fame" Inductee.

➤ **2008:** Indiana State House of Representatives 95th Legislative District Community Service Recognition.

➤ **2010:** To Date – over 500,000 volunteer man hours served.

➤ **2015:** College Mentors for Kids, Inspire Award Youth Mentor of the Year.

References

Benington, D.K., (2009) Kekionga Marker, Fort Wayne, Allen County, Indiana

http://www.ivanfraser.com/articles/conspiracie s/bigbrother.html

john freeman

www.accessgenealogy.com/african/tracts/more_victims.ht m

Lazzerini, R., (2006) *Index of Historical Reviews*, University of California, Santa Barbara

Motherjones.com/politics/2010/…/financial-crisis-wall-street-anger

Coffee, R. (1997). Cultural Diversity, In the Complete MBA Companion. *Pitman Publishing*. Retrieved May 29, 2008, from http://www.answers.com

Kelli, A., Lopez, M., Wysocki, A., & Kepner, K. (2008). Diversity in the Workplace Benefits Challenges and the Required Managerial Tools. *University of Florida IFAS Extension,* Retrieved May 29, 2008, from http://www.edis.ifas.ufl.edu

Alloggiamento, N. (1996, August). How to get a raise and some fabulous perks. *Cosmopolitan, 221* (2) 106.

Elliot, J., Smith, R.A. (2004, October). Workplace inequality common in United States study shows. *Black Issues in Higher Education, 21* (17) 10

Golden business ideas. (1998, June). *Journal of Business Accountancy, 191* (16) 124.

Lissy, W.E. (1995, March). Sexual favoritism. *Supervision, 56* (3) 18

Lotito, M., Valenza, G. (2005). California ruling on workplace romance sends employers scrambling for cover. *Venulex Legal Summaries*, pp1-2.

McKee, M. (2005, July). Court equates favoritism with discrimination. *The Recorder*, retrieved March 19, 2008, General one file. Gale. Apollo library

Reskin, B. (2005 1st quarter). Unconsciousness raising. *Regional Review, 14* (3) 32-37.

Samual, R., Singer, D. (2005, winter). Sexual favoritism. *Employee Relations Journal, 31* (3) 3-11.

Shaffer, D., Mays, P., Eththerige, K. (1976, October). Who shall be hired: A biasing effect of the Buckley amendment on employment practices. *Journal of Applied Psychology, 61* (5) 571

Sheridan, M. (2007, spring). Just because its sex, doesn't mean it's because of sex. *Columbia Journal of Law and Social Problems, 40* (3) 379

Maslow, A., (1954). Maslow's hierachy of needs. Retrieved September 19, 2008. From University of Phoenix E-bookCollection,https://ecampus.phoenix.edu

Carpenter, S., Huffman, K. (2008). Visualizing *Psychology: Personality. Retrieved September 19, 2008. From University of Phoenix E-book*

Collection,https://ecampus.phoenix.edu

Carpenter, S., Huffman, K. (2008). Visualizing Psychology: Life Span Development I. Retrieved September 19, 2008. From University of Phoenix E- book

Collection,https://ecampus.phoenix.edu

Jenkins, W.L. (2004). Understanding and Educating African American Children. William Jenkins Enterprises. p 17.

Dr. Canfield, Ken, National Center for Fathering, Retrieved October 11th, 2007

Indiana Center for Family, Schools & Community Partnerships, Retrieved October 11th, 2007

The National Fatherhood Institute, Retrieved October 11th, 2007

National P.T.A., State Parent & Teachers Association, Retrieved October 11th, 2007

Wallace I, Anthony, Security Dads Inc., Fathers Manual How To. Retrieved May 8th, 1999

Clemens, L. (2007). ESPN Walks the Walk on Screen and Off. Multichannel News. Retrieved May 30, 2008, from http://www.multichannel.com

Sweeney, J. (2008). Multicultural in the Workplace. John Sweeney Speaker. Retrieved May 30, 2008 from http://www.speedoflaughter.com

How Are We Transforming Education in Indianapolis. (2008). Retrieved May 10th, 2008, from http:// www.headlines.ips.k12.in.us

Corey, G., Corey, M.S. (2006). *I Never Knew I had a Choice*; *Explorations in Personal Growth* (8th ed.). Thomson Brooks/Cole

Kohlberg, L. (1984). *The Psychology of Moral Development: The Nature and Validity of Moral Stages (Essays on Moral Development, Volume 2).* Harper & Row

Piaget, J. (1932). *The moral judgment of the child.* London: Kegan Paul, Trench, Trubner & Co.

"A Cloud of Dust"

Security DAD Inc.

F. A. T. H. E. R.

www.ingramcontent.com/pod-product-compliance
Lightning Source LLC
Chambersburg PA
CBHW051836090426

42736CB00011B/1833